The Amazing
Kid Entrepreneur

By

Zohra Sarwari

Eman Publishing
P.O. Box 404
FISHERS, IN 46038
www.emanpublishing.com

Order Online: www.zohrasarwari.com

ISBN 13: 978-0-9841275-2-8
ISBN 10: 0-9841275-2-6
LCCN: 2010923208

EMAN
publishing

Cover Design by Zeeshan Shaikh

Printed in the United States of America

The Amazing
Kid Entrepreneur

By

Zohra Sarwari

Dedication

'(Our Lord! Accept this from us; You are the All-Hearing, the All-Knowing).'

(The Qur'aan: Chapter 2, Verse 127)

Acknowledgments

In the name of the Allaah, the Most Gracious, the Most Magnificent. All praise is due to Allaah, Lord of the universe. We praise Him, and seek His help and His forgiveness, and we seek His protection from the accursed Satan. Whomever Allaah guides will never be misguided, and whomever He allows to be misguided will never be guided. I bear witness that there is no deity worthy of worship except Allaah, who is One; alone, and has no partners. I bear witness that Muhammad is His servant and messenger. May the blessings of Allaah be upon him, his family, his companions, and the righteous that follow them, until the Day of Judgment.

I would like to thank my family and friends for all of their support, especially Zeeshan, Madeeha, and Saqib Shaikh, who are an asset to my team *masha'Allaah.– jazaakum-Allaahu khayran -* May Allaah (SWT) reward you all - *aameen!*

Terminology

1. **"ALLAAH"** is the Arabic name for THE ONE SUPREME UNIVERSAL GOD.
2. **"SWT"** is an abbreviation of the Arabic words, *"Subhaanahu wa Ta'ala"* which means "Glory Be To Him".
3. **Al-Qur'aan:** The Book of Allaah; divine guidance for mankind; the FINAL TESTAMENT.
4. **Muslim** is one who has submitted to the Will of ALLAAH.
5. **Allaahu-Akbar** means ALLAAH is the Greatest.
6. **Assalaamu-alaykum** means 'Peace be upon you.' It is a greeting among the Muslims. The response to this greeting is **'Wa 'alaykum assalaam**,' which means 'And Peace be upon you'.
7. **Hajj** is one of the five pillars of Islam, a duty one must perform during one's life-time if one has the financial resources for it. It must be performed during certain specified dates of Dhul-Hijjah.
8. **PBUH** means Peace Be Upon Him.
9. **Alhamdulillaah** means Praise be to ALLAAH!
10. **Wudoo** means ablution.
11. **5 Daily Prayers (Salaah):**
    1. ***Fajr (pre-dawn):*** This prayer starts off the day with the remembrance of Allaah (SWT); it is performed before sunrise.
    2. ***Dhuhr (noon):*** After the day's work has begun, one breaks shortly after noon to again remember Allaah (SWT) and seek His guidance.
    3. ***'Asr (afternoon):*** In the late afternoon, people are usually busy wrapping up the day's work, getting kids home from school, etc. It is an important time to take a few minutes to remember Allaah (SWT) and the greater meaning of our lives.
    4. ***Maghrib (sunset):*** Just after the sun goes down, Muslims remember Allaah (SWT) again as the day comes to a close.
    5. ***'Isha (evening):*** Before retiring for the night, Muslims again take time to remember Allaah (SWT)'s presence, guidance, mercy, and forgiveness.
12. **Du'aa** is supplication in Islam.
13. **Insha'Allaah** means 'If Allaah Wills'.

14. Hadith means the actions and sayings of Prophet Muhammad (PBUH), reported by his companions, and collected by scholars who came after them, in books.

15. Surah refers to a chapter in the Qur'aan.

16. Iqaamah means the second call to Islamic prayer, given immediately before the prayer begins

17. Hijaab refers to the women's dress code in this book.

18. Subhaan'Allaah means "Glory to Allaah".

19. Dhikr means remembering and commemorating ALLAAH.

20. Prophet Muhammad (SAAW) Here SAAW is an abbreviation for 'Salallaahu alayhi wa sallam' and it means, 'May Allaah's Peace and Praise be upon him' in Arabic.

21. Ramadan is the ninth month of the Islamic calendar. It is the Islamic month of fasting, in which Muslims refrain from eating, drinking, smoking, from dawn until sunset.

22. Eid means celebration. There are two official Eids in Islam and they are Eid al-fitr (Celebration of the feast of breaking fast at the end of Ramadhan) and Eid al-Adhha (Islamic-dictionary.com). Eld Al-Fitr and Eld Al-Adhaa are two Islaamic festivals. The first occurs at the end of the fasting month of Ramadhaan, whilst the second occurs at the end of the Hajj.

23. Ameen is an Arabic word which means, 'O Allaah, answer my supplication.

24. AstaghfirUllaah An Arabic phrase meaning "I ask Allah forgiveness."

25. Sadaqah means Charity. Often, sadaqah is given out of personal reasons to whomever the giver deems suitable, e.g. a local charity shop. Giving sadaqah is given irrespective of the compulsory taxes and doesn't count as zakat - zakat must be payed irrelevent of the amount spent in sadaqah (Islamic-dictionary.com).

Table of Contents

Chapter 1

Lina's Special Project

BEEP BEEP BEEP!

Lina rolled over and looked at her alarm clock: 6 o'clock already! She looked over at Qadeer who was still snoring lightly. She shook him, *"Qadeer, time to get up."* Then she pulled herself out of bed and grabbed her robe from the closet. She squinted her eyes so she was not blinded by the light and flipped on the hall light. Down the hall was Yasmine's room; Lina and Qadeer had been married almost 8 years, and Yasmine was their pride and joy. Six years old and full of life, she was both kind and feisty. She also was not a morning person.

"Yasmine, time to get up, honey."

There was some incoherent mumbling under the covers which rustled slightly. Lina walked to the bed and sat down. She gently rubbed Yasmine's back and pulled back the covers. Yasmine glared up at her mother and sighed deeply. Lina couldn't help but laugh. No matter how bad her mood, Yasmine always looked a little too sweet to pull off the angry look effectively.

"Mom, why do I have to get up so early?" Yasmine asked.

"Because it is Fajr salaah, and you need to get ready and have breakfast before the bus comes. You know that. Now say your morning du'aas, get dressed, make wudoo and hurry downstairs." Lina stood up and walked to the door.

"Assalaamu-alaykum, Mom..."

Lina turned around and saw Yasmine sitting up in bed now. She smiled broadly and said, *"Wa'alaykum-assalaam. I'll see you downstairs in a minute."*

Once Lina had changed and walked downstairs, she found Qadeer waiting for his wife and daughter. He had already rolled out his prayer mat so it was facing northeast, and he was sitting on the couch remembering Allaah by doing *dhikr*. When he saw Lina, he looked up and smiled.

"Assalaamu-alaykum!" Qadeer patted the couch next to him. *"Did you sleep well?"*

Lina smiled at Qadeer. *"Alhamdulillaah,"* she said as she sat down beside him. There was a loud thump and the ceiling fan rattled above them. Lina sighed as Yasmine came running down the stairs.

"I'm ready!" she exclaimed breathlessly. Yasmine had already perfected the art of creating a grand entrance.

"Alhamdulillaah!" said Qadeer. *"Then let us begin."* Qadeer stood on his prayer mat as Lina and Yasmine stood behind him. He then recited the *iqaamah*, and began leading the prayer. At the conclusion of the prayer they all sat and recited their *dhikr* and *du'aas*. As they were done they rolled up their prayer mats. *"Allaahu Akbar,"* Lina said. *"Now let's go have breakfast!"*

After breakfast Lina cleared the plates while Yasmine grabbed her backpack. *"Can I have $10, Mom?"*

"What on earth do you need $10 for?" Lina looked at her daughter perplexed.

"There is a book fair at school. I want to buy a book." Yasmine looked up at her mom with pleading eyes.

"Honey, your dad works hard for his money. You can't expect to get everything you want. We just paid $5 last week for your recorder for Qur'aan class last week, and we agreed to buy you hot lunch next week." Lina sighed as Yasmine continued to stare with wide eyes. She reluctantly reached for her purse and pulled out her wallet. *"Okay, you can have $10, but we really need to think of a better way to handle all your money requests."*

Yasmine smiled brightly and thanked her mom as she took the money. Then, she hopped up and planted a kiss on Lina's cheek before running out the door.

With Qadeer off to work and Yasmine on her way to school, Lina had the house to herself. Although she loved the company of her husband and daughter, there was something particularly satisfying about this time of day. The house was quiet, and she could be alone in her thoughts. As she began to load the dishwasher, Lina considered what to do with Yasmine.

Although only 6, Yasmine was a precocious child. Maybe it was the result of being an only child, but regardless, she always seemed wise beyond her years. Lina smiled to herself as she thought of Yasmine's never-ending questions about Allaah, the daily news and just about everything else under the sun. *"Alhamdulillaah,"* she said quietly under her breath.

Then her thoughts turned to the book fair money, and her smile disappeared. This was only the second month of school and already she felt like she was being nickel-and-dimed at every turn. Lina had always expected that the first grade would bring added expenses, but Yasmine's requests had become more and more frequent.

Fortunately, Qadeer had a good job as an accountant so the money itself wasn't the problem; but Lina was worried that Yasmine didn't really grasp the concept behind the money. She was constantly asking for $2 here and $5 there. Lina couldn't help but feel that her daughter was beginning to see her as an endless supply of cash; simply ask and receive.

Lina grabbed the laundry hamper and headed down to the washing machine, deep in thought. It was certainly a problem. She didn't want to deny Yasmine…after all, what are a couple of bucks once in a while? As she emptied in the laundry detergent, she shook her head. No, Lina thought, the question shouldn't be about denying or indulging Yasmine, it should be about teaching her responsibility. After all, what will happen once she's an adult, and she is used to having everything handed to her? That wouldn't be fair either.

With the laundry started, Lina returned to the kitchen and sat at the table. She lowered her head into her hands and asked for guidance from Allaah. There was certainly a solution to this dilemma; it just needed to be revealed to her.

"Insha'Allaah!" Lina jerked her head up when inspiration hit. Of course! How simple! Yasmine could simply earn her own money to spend as she wished.

Lina stood up quickly and headed upstairs to the bedroom. Once there, she reached for the change jar that sat on her end table. Dumping its contents on the bed, she searched for several coins before returning the rest of the money to the jar. Then she returned to the kitchen table and pulled out her purse. From her wallet, Lina removed several bills and set them on the table with the change.

Looking around, Lina searched with her eyes for what else she would need. When she couldn't find it, she walked down to the basement. In the recycling box, she found just what she wanted. She pulled out some clean aluminum cans and set them aside. Then she spied the empty glass jars. These would be better she thought; Yasmine would be able to see what is inside.

Returning upstairs, Lina inspected the jars to make sure each was completely clean. She lined the four jars on the table, next to the change and bills which she spread out. Now all that was needed was to wait for Yasmine to get home.

It was a gorgeous October day. The type that looks like it came right out of a home and garden magazine. The bright green of the trees had given way to hues of deep red, yellow and orange. The air was crisp and a light wind rustled fallen leaves down the sidewalk. Most of the neighborhood homes had fall decorations such as pumpkins or scarecrows gracing their front porches or steps. Lina stood by the kitchen counter and took in the scene out of the window as she pulled out the dinner ingredients.

"Bye, Courtney! See you tomorrow!" With a slam, the front door announced the arrival of Yasmine. *"Assalaamu-alaykum, Mom!"* she said, as she slung her backpack over the back of a chair. The words tumbled out of her mouth, *"You'll never believe what happened today. Grace brought her cat – he's huge! – brought her cat to show 'n tell. He made Ali sneeze because Ali is allergic, but I was able to hold him, and he was all fuzzy. Oh and we're going on a field trip to an orchard…I have the permission slip here…we're going to see how apples grow and how they're picked and how they make them into apple juice. Did you know that apples are nature's toothbrush?"*

Lina laughed quietly under her breath. That was her Yasmine. Always talking and always thinking. *"Yes, yes, my love. It sounds like you have had a full day. We'll talk more at dinner when your father is home – insha'Allaah. For now, put away your things."*

Yasmine removed her coat and placed it in the closet. She also took out her school folder and handed it to her mother.

"Do you have any homework?" Lina always asked but knew the answer would always be the same.

"We had a math page to do, but I finished my spelling earlier and did the math in school. It's in my folder."

Lina scanned the sheet to make sure it had been finished correctly before setting it aside. She also looked over the other school sheets Yasmine had brought home and made a note of the field trip date. It did sound like fun, and Lina hoped she would have the chance to chaperone.

"Now, go upstairs and change your clothes, make wudoo, and get ready for the afternoon prayer – 'Asr salaah." Yasmine ran upstairs to change, and make wudoo. Lina went to the living room and set up the prayer rugs, put on her prayer clothes, and was reciting Qur'aan while Yasmine was getting ready for 'Asr prayer.

After prayer, Lina sat on the couch while Yasmine recited a section of the Qur'aan. Lina's mother had made sure that Lina had memorized the entire Qur'aan by age 15. Although she didn't really appreciate it at the time, Lina had come to realize what a blessing it was to have such intimate knowledge of Allaah's (SWT) Word. It had given her comfort and wisdom so many times; so she had made it a priority to help Yasmine learn it as well.

"It is God who has made the earth a resting-place for you and the sky a canopy, and has formed you - and formed you so well and provided for you sustenance out of the good things of life. Such is God, your Sustainer: hallowed, then, is God, the Sustainer of all the worlds!"

(Qur'aan, Chapter 40: Verse 64)

Yasmine had been working on this verse, reciting it in Arabic for the past week and had it almost perfect. Lina smiled and clapped her hands together. *"Allaahu Akbar! Beautiful, Yasmine. I think you are ready to move on to the next verse."*

She stood up and walked to the kitchen. Yasmine followed and pulled out some paperwork from a desk in the hall.

"Do you need some help with your Arabic today?" Lina asked.

"No, I am still doing these review sheets," Yasmine answered.

"Okay, well let me know when they are done, and I'll go over the next lesson with you." Lina walked to the counter and continued her dinner preparation while Yasmine reviewed her Arabic lessons. Later, they would work on her Islamic studies.

Usually, Lina was able to time their lessons so that they would be complete at just about the same time Qadeer arrived home from work; and today was no exception. Yasmine was putting away her notebook and pencil when her dad walked in.

"Assaalamu-alaykum, Daddy!"

"Wa'alaykum assalaam wa rahmat-Ullaahi wa barakaatuhu - Yasmine – and how was my princess' day?" Qadeer bent over to kiss Yasmine before setting down his briefcase.

"Alhamdulillaah! I got to hold Grace's cat and we're going to an orchard to see how apple juice is made!" Yasmine beamed at her dad.

He ruffled her hair and smiled down at her, "Sounds like fun!"

"Yasmine, time to do your chores," Lina interrupted. "Will you please make sure all your dirty laundry is in the wash room, and then you can set the table for dinner."

As Yasmine ran off to her room, Qadeer greeted Lina. He looked down at the table and saw the line up of jars and change. "What's all this?" he asked.

"Oh! I completely forgot! That's my special project for Yasmine and me later." Lina smiled secretly, and Qadeer raised an eyebrow in response.

"Okay, well, I'll leave you girls to your fun. I'm going to go up and get changed." Qadeer walked upstairs and left Lina smiling to herself about what the future might hold.

After dinner, Yasmine helped her mother clear up the dining room table. They packed up the leftovers and ran the dishwasher. Lina sent Yasmine outside to play before the day's sun slipped away and sat down with Qadeer to discuss his day. She also told him about her plan for Yasmine. He nodded in agreement and said that it was a fine idea. Satisfied that they were on the same page, Lina called Yasmine inside and put her plan into action.

Sitting at the table, Lina pointed out the coins and bills. "Now, I know you know about money right, Yasmine?" She nodded in response. "So why don't you go ahead and arrange these coins and bills into the order of how much they are worth."

Yasmine picked up the bills and quickly set them in order. Then she took the coins in her hand. She carefully considered the coins before setting them down; penny, dime, nickel and quarter.

"Close, but not quite...See even though the dime is small, it is worth 10 cents. The nickel looks bigger but it is only worth 5 cents," Lina explained, as she switched the order of the coins. "Can you tell me why we need money, Yasmine?"

"To buy stuff."

"That's right. A long time ago, people used to barter for what they needed. So someone with chickens might trade eggs for some milk from a neighbor's cow. But over time, it became easier just to use money instead. And all money has a value. That means that people don't just give it away. Do you understand what I mean?"

Lina wasn't sure if Yasmine was following her. She seemed to be more interested in staring at her fingernails than anything else, but then she looked up and said, *"Yeah. It's like how Daddy goes to work each day. His boss pays him for the work he does. Instead of Dad trading eggs for milk, he is trading work for money. Is that right?"*

"That's a good way of looking at it," Lina said. *"So that means that every time you need money your dad has to work for it. Oh, and that reminds me…did you get your book at school?"*

Yasmine's eyes lit up. She nodded her head vigorously and jumped up from the table. She ran to her room and came back with a glossy book about cats. *"Isn't it cool, Mom? It tells you all about the different cats and how to take care of them!"*

Lina smiled, *"Yes, what a nice book, but remember that your dad had to work hard to get the money to buy this book."* Lina set the book aside to make sure Yasmine wasn't distracted. *"I thought it might be nice if you had your own money to spend so you won't have to ask us for money."*

"Like an allowance?!" Yasmine practically knocked her chair over. *"Omar gets $5 a week, and he can spend it on anything he wants. So you mean like that?"*

"Well, not quite. See, no one will just give me money to spend and no one will give your dad money to spend. Like you said earlier, Dad has to trade his work for money. So I am thinking that we can have you trade some work for money as well. Think of it as your first job. You'll still have to do your regular chores, but we can find some extra work that you can do, and I'll pay you for each job. And we can work it out so that the harder the job, the more money you can earn. How does that sound to you?"

Nodding her head quickly, there was no doubt that Yasmine loved this idea. Lina could see the wheels in her head turning as she thought about all that she could buy with "her money". Together, they drafted a list of possible chores and the appropriate "wage" to go along with each job.

Job	Wage
Fold Laundry	$2.00
Change Clothes in Washer	$1.00
Help Make Dinner	$1.00
Rake Leaves	$2.50
Scrub Toilet (Ew!)	$3.50
Take Out Trash	$3.00

"Insha'Allaah – I think that is a good start!" Lina said, as she put down her pen. "Now, there is just one other matter to discuss." She moved the glass jars in front of Yasmine.

"What are those for?" Yasmine asked.

"These are your 'banks'. When you save up a little money, we can open a real account at the bank, but these will do for now. Let's say our car breaks down; how do you think we pay for it?" Lina paused to look at Yasmine who clearly had no clue.

She continued, "We take money out of our savings. And how do we get money in our savings? Well, we make sure we don't spend everything your dad makes each week. We set some aside in case we have an emergency or if we want to buy something that is expensive. A lot of people call it a 'Rainy Day Fund'."

Yasmine nodded at this. "But I won't have to worry about a car breaking down. I can't drive yet," Yasmine said, matter-of-factly.

Lina laughed lightly. "Alhamdulillaah! How right you are, Yasmine! But that doesn't mean you shouldn't save some of your money. You never know when you'll have an emergency or what type it will be. And you also want to save if there is something big you want to buy. That's what your father and I did when we wanted to buy a new couch. It was too much money to just pay for without planning. So we set aside a little each week until we had enough. Is there something you want, Yasmine?"

"A cat!" Yasmine exclaimed. Lina should have known; Yasmine adored cats. "I want an American Bobtail! They are so pretty and they have these cute little tails."

"Okay, you want a cat. An American Bobtail will not be cheap. And then you have to pay for all its supplies and take it to the vet and you can end up spending a lot of money on a cat." Lina marked a piece of masking tape with the word "Savings" and placed it on the jar. "If you want a cat, Yasmine, you will need to save for it."

Lina pulled out the second jar. "Now, Yasmine, can you tell me the 5 pillars of Islam?"

Yasmine was so excited about the cat that she hadn't prepared herself for a question about Islam. It took her a minute to collect herself and think. She started slowly while trying to remember her lessons. "To worship only One God…to pray…to, ah… to observe Ramadan, to make a pilgrimage to Makkah…and to give to charity," Yasmine beamed, knowing that she had remembered them all. Lina smiled in return.

"Very good! Now there are two pillars that can be assigned to two of these jars. Which do you think they are?"

After a moment of thought, Yasmine rightly answered that one jar could be used for money for charity. However, she was stuck on the next jar. Finally, she had to ask her mom for help. Lina explained, "Remember what I said about saving for expensive things? Like how you want to save for a cat?" Yasmine nodded. "Well, one of the most important things for every Muslim is to make a pilgrimage to Makkah (Hajj); but going on the Hajj is very expensive. The plane ticket alone could be a thousand dollars. Since this is such an important thing and it costs so much money, many Muslims have separate savings just for this trip. So we can make this jar your Hajj account. Okay?"

Yasmine nodded and agreed that it was a good idea. She picked up the last jar and asked her mom, "Then what's this one for?"

"That's the fun jar!" Lina smiled. "That's the jar which has the money for you to spend on whatever you want!" Yasmine smiled and bounced in her seat. Lina looked over her shoulder and out the window. "The sun is setting, time for Maghrib salaah. We'd better hurry; your father is probably waiting."

As they walked to the living room, Yasmine gave her mom's waist a squeeze. Lina put her arm around her daughter and smiled. Today had been a productive day; alhamdulillaah!

Chapter 2

Yasmine's First Purchase

Sydney stared at Yasmine with wide eyes as she pulled a small wad of bills from her pocket. The girl with light curls and big blue eyes stood staring at the money as Yasmine counted each bill. *"You have a lot of money!"* she said breathlessly.

Yasmine smiled broadly. It really wasn't that much; she had a lot more at home, but she didn't want to brag. So she said, *"I've been saving for a while."*

Pulling at her blond curls, Sydney leaned over to get a better look. *"But you have a 5 dollar…can I see?"* She held out her hand and looked expectantly at Yasmine who placed the bill in her hand.

As Sydney examined the money, Yasmine turned her attention back to the display of school items adorning the back corner of the office. Since starting school she had always wanted her own Maple Valley t-shirt. It had the school name and a picture of a cougar that was the school mascot. Each night Yasmine had carefully counted the money in her "fun jar" at home. Even though the t-shirt was only $10, she didn't want to spend all her money on it; so she was waiting until she had $20 in her home bank.

This morning she had carefully taken out a $5 bill and 5 $1 bills and folded them tightly. She placed them in her pocket and stopped by the school's Spirit Store as soon as she got to school. The Spirit Store was actually just a section of the main office. Mrs. Newman, the secretary would help students who wanted to buy something. During conferences, the items would be moved out to the hall for parents who wanted to buy something. There were bumper stickers, pencils and sweatshirts, but Yasmine had her eye on the long sleeve t-shirt.

"You should get the sweatshirt – it's December," Sydney piped up, handing back the $5 bill. She looked longingly at a bright pink sweatshirt that said "Maple Valley School".

"I know its December, but I want something I can wear all year. That t-shirt," she pointed to one high on the wall, *"has long sleeves so I can wear it in the winter. And it's light enough that I can wear it in the summer. It's $10 cheaper too!"* Yasmine smiled broadly at Sydney.

"Hmmmm," Sydney shrugged, still staring at the sweatshirt.

"Are you all set, honey?" Mrs. Newman walked from a backroom into the office.

Yasmine nodded vigorously. *"I want that shirt."* She pointed to the long-sleeved t-shirt with the cougar and laid out the bills on Mrs. Newman's desk.

"Okay," Mrs. Newman said, as she walked to a back cupboard. *"I think we'll get you a size medium."* She pulled out a shirt and turned towards Yasmine. Holding it up, she looked at the shirt and looked at Yasmine. *"Yes, I think this is the right size for you. It might be a touch big right now, but then you can wear it through next year too. Does that sound all right?"*

Yasmine agreed and reached for the shirt as Mrs. Newman counted her money. *"It was nice of your mom and dad to buy you the shirt, Yasmine. I know you've wanted it for a while."*

"Oh, my parents aren't buying it, Mrs. Newman," Yasmine said. Mrs. Newman looked up in surprise. *"I'm buying this with money from my business."*

"Your business?" Mrs. Newman asked.

"Yup, I have a home cleaning business. I help my mom around the house, and I get paid for the chores. The really yucky stuff like cleaning the toilet gets me the most money, but I've learned how to do it really quick so it's not too bad. I have another $10 in my fun jar at home, and I'm saving up for a cat and a trip to Makkah too – insha'Allaah!" Yasmine stopped breathlessly, as Mrs. Newman put away the money in a cash box.

"That's nice, honey. Enjoy your shirt. And you'd better get to class – the bell will ring soon. You too, Sydney," Mrs. Newman shooed them out of the office, and the girls ran down the hall laughing together.

At dinner that night Yasmine pulled out her new shirt to show her mom and dad.

"How wonderful!" Lina said. *"Your first purchase with **your** money!"*

Yasmine practically jumped out of her chair with excitement. *"I'm going to wear it to school tomorrow. I wanted to change in the bathroom today, but I didn't have time before the bell rang."* She beamed from ear to ear. Then she added, *"Sydney was soooo jealous. She couldn't believe all the money I had!"*

Lina and Qadeer exchanged glances. *"Yes, you are becoming quite the wealthy young lady,"* Qadeer said to Yasmine. *"But let us remember that all we have comes from Allaah (SWT), and we don't want to be boastful about our blessings. As Allaah's creation we must always strive to be humble and compassionate towards others."*

The smile disappeared from Yasmine's face. *"I'm sorry, Dad. I forgot."* Then the smile returned. *"Maybe I could buy Sydney the pink sweatshirt she wants as a gift!"*

Lina could see Yasmine was already working out the plan in her mind. She could only imagine what grand way Yasmine would unveil the sweatshirt and surprise Sydney. She rubbed her daughter's back and laughed. *"Alhamdulillaah! That is a wonderfully generous idea, Yasmine. Although I imagine the sweatshirt is quite expensive, but if that doesn't work out, maybe you can buy her something else that she might like?"*

Yasmine beamed at her mom.

Qadeer motioned his hands interrupting and said, *"Yasmine, why don't you get the dishes cleared off the table and then you can read for a while before Maghrib salaah."*

Lina helped Yasmine pick up the dishes and wrap the leftovers. Once everything had been loaded up into the dishwasher, Yasmine added soap and turned the machine on. Then she ran to her room to read; she was in the middle of an exciting book about a cat that had been left behind on a camping trip. When she left off last a thunderstorm had just begun and the cat was stuck on a log near a rising river. Yasmine had wanted to continue the book, but her mom called her for *Maghrib salaah*. So Yasmine put the book away. She ran down the stairs to get her prayer clothes on.

After her *salaah*, Yasmine ran back upstairs to continue reading; it was time to see if the cat would be washed away or safely make it to shore.

After Yasmine had left, Lina and Qadeer sat down together at the table. Lina always cherished these quiet moments late in the day. All the chores were done, and it was time to simply enjoy her family. Qadeer's job as an accountant always led to some interesting stories, but there were also heartbreaking tales of small businesses who were destined for bankruptcy because of poor planning and too much debt. It always saddened Lina to hear how some people's dreams were shattered simply because they tried to start their business quick with large loans instead of saving slowly.

"Do you worry that you are pushing her too fast?" Qadeer's question interrupted Lina's thoughts. She looked at her husband

questioningly. *"Yasmine,"* he clarified. *"Do you think this 'cleaning business' is too much too soon for her?"*

Lina shook her head. *"No because we haven't forced her into anything. I introduced the idea, and she loved it. If she didn't, I wouldn't make her continue."* Lina stopped and looked off in the distance as she collected her thoughts.

"I suppose you're right," Qadeer agreed.

"Insha'Allaah, I think Allaah has great plans for our Yasmine. She is such a bright girl – masha'Allaah." Lina smiled to herself before looking up at Qadeer again. *"I know that sounds conceited...perhaps I have to work on my humility as well."*

"No," Qadeer said. *"I think you are stating a fact. There is certainly something about Yasmine. She has such an independent spirit and when she puts her mind to something, well, there really is no stopping her - alhamdulillaah."*

Lina was relieved that Qadeer saw it as well. In many ways, Yasmine was just a normal, fun child, but in others, she seemed wise and mature beyond her years. *"Allaahu Akbar,"* Lina said softly under her breath. Then she said, *"But we must be sure that we nurture her creativity and confidence without letting her become self-absorbed or arrogant. I would hate to see our lovely daughter forget that all good things come from Allaah and Allaah alone."*

Qadeer nodded in agreement and then looked out the window. *"It is about time for our Isha prayer. Will you please call down Yasmine while I get the prayer mats?"*

After *salaah*, both parents stood and left the room together. Tonight's prayer would have an especially important meaning for both of them as they praised Allaah for His gift of Yasmine and asked for His Guidance in leading her in His Ways.

The next day of school Yasmine was barely into the classroom before she had her coat off and was saying 'Hi' to Mrs. Chrisman. The young first grade teacher had barely turned in time to see the blur that was Yasmine running back to the hall to hang up her coat. But a moment later the excited girl appeared in the doorway again.

Mrs. Chrisman was probably one of the nicest people Yasmine knew...other than her mother of course. Her dark brown *hijaab* was nicely pinned, and her eyes always seemed to twinkle. Best of all, she listened intently to every word Yasmine said; even if it was the tenth time she had heard about the American Bobtail named Ally that Yasmine would someday own, she listened with rapt attention as if it were the first time she had heard of it. Unlike Mrs. Newman or some of the other teachers who seemed distracted when she talked, Yasmine could always count on Mrs. Chrisman to listen.

"Aha! The long awaited shirt!" Mrs. Chrisman walked briskly to Yasmine. *"Let me see,"* she said. As she twirled her hand, Yasmine spun around. *"It looks great!"*

Mrs. Chrisman knew all about Yasmine's work at home and the money she was earning. She also knew that the shirt was the first thing that Yasmine had her eye on when it came time to spend some of that money.

A blonde head peeked in the door. It was Sydney. Although in kindergarten, Sydney had firmly attached herself to Yasmine, and Yasmine didn't mind. Sydney was happy to do whatever she had in mind and was always bright and bubbly. Unlike some of the other girls, she wasn't too concerned with what was considered "cool". That was definitely welcoming for Yasmine who had encountered some problems with kids who didn't seem to understand why she didn't watch TV, eat bacon, or go to church with them on Sunday.

"Let me see, Yasmine!" Sydney squealed. Yasmine turned to the door and struck a pose. Sydney giggled in delight. *"You look great…but I still would have gotten the pink sweatshirt."* And as quickly as she arrived, Sydney skipped down the hall to her room.

Mrs. Chrisman laughed. *"Sydney sure loves pink, doesn't she?"* Yasmine nodded in agreement. *"But I like this one for you. It has the picture of the cougar on it which is perfect for you."*

"That's what I thought too!" said Yasmine. She looked down at her shirt and smiled yet again.

"So, what's next on the agenda?" asked Mrs. Chrisman. Yasmine looked up not understanding. *"I mean, what do you want to buy next with the money you are earning?"*

Yasmine's face lit up with understanding. *"I'm not sure what I'll get myself, but I am going to buy the pink sweatshirt in the office for Sydney."*

"That's very nice of you, Yasmine. Sydney is fortunate…"

"Mrs. Chrisman, where did I put my papers?" Brett interrupted them.

"Shhhh…," Mrs. Chrisman scolded Brett lightly. *"Please wait your turn."* She turned back to Yasmine. *"We'll talk later. Okay?"*

Yasmine agreed and headed to her desk as the classroom began to fill with other students.

'The Prophet Muhammad (SAAW) received the Word of Allaah (SWT) from the Angel Gabriel (PBUH) in the 7ᵗʰ century. Muhammad (SAAW) was Allaah's last prophet. Allaah's Word is the Qur'aan.'

Although Yasmine's reading skills were advanced, she still had to work hard on her handwriting. She concentrated deeply on each word as she wrote out her Islamic studies lesson. After finishing the answer, she paused for a moment and became lost in thought; she wondered what it must have been like for the Prophet Muhammad (SAAW). Did he (SAAW) know he was special? Was he (SAAW) scared when the Angel appeared to him?

As her thoughts wandered from Allaah (SWT) to the Prophet Muhammad (SAAW), she began to wonder how she could give honor to Allaah in her life. She was only 6…well, almost 7. There probably wasn't much she could do. But no, it wasn't really a good excuse to say she was too young; lots of kids did great things when they were young.

"Earth to Yasmine!" startled out of her thoughts, Yasmine jumped slightly. Lina peered over the table at her paper. *"That looks good. Are you stuck on the next answer?"*

"No, Mom. I was just thinking about how the Prophet Muhammad (SAAW) was picked to do something great by Allaah (SWT). And I was just thinking that it would be nice if I could do something great for Allaah too," Yasmine explained.

Lina nodded. *"Alhamdulillaah. I'm glad to hear that you are thinking these things, Yasmine. We must make du'aa (supplicate) to Allaah (SWT) to see if He can help you determine how best to glorify Him."*

Yasmine nodded. *"I was also thinking about my business."* She looked up at her mom. *"Mrs. Chrisman asked me today, what is the next thing I want to buy with my money. You know, I've been thinking all day, and I'm not sure what I want to buy. I am saving for the cat and for my pilgrimage to Makkah, and I think that's really all I want right now."* She paused for a moment before continuing. *"I was also thinking about how excited Sydney will be when I buy her* the sweatshirt, and I would love to be able to help other people with my money too."

"I understand, Yasmine. That's one of the wonderful things about money. It not only buys you a roof over your head and food to put on the table, but it also allows you to be generous with others. Much good can be done with money, so long as you do not allow it to control you." Lina sat down at the table. "Maybe it's time for you to create a business plan."

"What's a business plan?"

"Well, a business plan gives all the details of a business and how it is going to make money. But it also gives your business a purpose. Every successful business has one. When I suggested that you start doing chores for money, I wasn't sure how seriously you'd take it," Lina smiled at Yasmine. "But now that you seem to have really taken it to heart, I think it may be time to write down something more formal. Finish up your Islamic studies now, and after dinner I'll work with you on the plan."

Once dinner and dishes were done, Yasmine and her mother sat at the table again. Lina laid out a paper and pencil in front of Yasmine. "I'll let you write. It will help with your handwriting too."

Yasmine sighed slightly but picked up the pencil. She looked at her mom expectantly. "What do I write?"

"Well, let's talk about it first," Lina said, and Yasmine put down the pencil. "Normally a business plan will include a mission statement; that says what your business does and why. Then it includes the business location, how much you have in expenses…"

"What are expenses?" Yasmine interrupted.

"Expenses are things you might have to buy to make your business work."

"But I don't have to buy anything, right?" Yasmine interrupted again.

Lina looked slightly exasperated. "Yes, if you'd let me finish, I could tell you. For a cleaning business, an expense might be cleaning supplies such as a mop or soap or washcloths. But I already have everything here for you to clean so you don't have any expenses right now."

"Okay," Yasmine understood.

Lina continued, "So a business plan will have a mission statement, the business location, expenses and expected revenues." Lina put up her hand to stop Yasmine before she interrupted again. *"Revenues are the money you make. So every time I pay you for a chore that is your business revenue."*

"So expenses are money you spend, and revenues are money you make?" Yasmine confirmed.

"That's right," Lina said. *"The final piece of your business plan is your profits. Profits are how much money you make minus the money you had to spend. That's your profit. Even if you have a lot of revenue, if you only have small profits, your business won't last long. Do you understand?"*

Yasmine looked confused. *"I think,"* she said.

Lina could tell that she didn't. *"Here,"* she took out a second piece of paper and wrote:

$10 (Revenue/Money Made)
- $7 (Expenses/Money Spent)

$3 (Profits/Yours to Spend)

"See," said Lina as she pointed to what she wrote. *"Let's pretend you have expenses for a moment. Now, let's imagine you've done enough chores to earn $10 from me, but you had to spend $7 on toilet bowl cleaner and a mop. So, that means that you really only have $3 left to spend."* Lina looked at Yasmine. *"I know it's hard to understand…"*

"No, I think I understand, Mom," Yasmine said. *"So even if you give me $10, I didn't really make $10 if I had to spend money to get the money…right?"*

"Sounds like you've got it, Yasmine!" Lina smiled at her daughter. *"So I think we are ready to start writing your business plan. Let's start with the mission statement…"*

Lina and Yasmine worked intently, stopping only for *Isha* prayer. Then they returned to the table to finish their work. When they were done it was Yasmine's bedtime and she gave a big yawn as she pushed away from the table.

"I'm sorry you didn't get a chance to read tonight, Yasmine," Lina apologized, but Yasmine shook her head.

"No, I'm glad we did this. It makes me feel good to know that I have a plan for my business. I can finish my book tomorrow." Yasmine leaned over to give her mom a kiss, and Lina hugged her

in return. With the work done Yasmine's business plan was left on the table to be implemented the next day...

Yasmine's House Cleaning Service

Mission Statement:
To provide exceptional house cleaning services at an affordable rate. Yasmine's House Cleaning Service exists to give glory to Allaah. By using God-given talents, Yasmine will seek out new opportunities to serve Allaah and help His people.

Business Location:
Currently at home; in the future, may expand to clean other homes.

Expenses:
None at this time – may use some advertising in future if expanding.

Revenues:
Varies depending on the service.

Profit:
Goal is to earn $10 per week to start, increase to $20 per week by March.

Chapter 3

Achieving A Goal

The smell of pancakes and eggs wafted up to Yasmine's room. She rolled over and squinted at the light streaming through the windows. She had slept late this morning. Normally, on the weekends she would stay up after Fajr prayer, but on this day she had decided to go back to bed.

Now she sat up and rubbed the sleep out of her eyes. She recited her morning *du'aas* as she was thinking in her bed. She had turned 7 last month but decided that she didn't feel a bit different than she did at 6. She swung her feet over the side of the bed and leaped to the floor. In the hallway she could hear her parents talking in the kitchen downstairs. Yasmine ran from the bathroom back to her room and pulled out her favorite pair of jeans. She rummaged through her dresser until she found the perfect shirt; dressy but not too fancy.

In the kitchen, Lina and Qadeer both looked up at the ceiling upon hearing the familiar stomping and rattling that normally accompanied Yasmine when she woke up. They smiled at one another before returning to their conversation. A minute later, Yasmine appeared. Her hair was pulled back in a loose ponytail at the base of her neck, and she had obviously put some thought into her outfit.

"Assalaamu-alaykum, my dear! You have decided to grace us with your presence, I see," Qadeer beamed at his daughter.

"Assalaamu-alaykum, honey," Lina leaned over for a kiss. *"I made your favorite – apple cinnamon pancakes and scrambled eggs."*

The family sat down together as the steaming food was placed at the center of the table. At Yasmine's place, a brightly wrapped package was decked out with ribbons and a card. Yasmine sat down and looked expectantly at her parents. *"It's the 6 month anniversary of your business,"* Lina explained. *"You've been so wrapped up in working hard that it doesn't seem you ever take the time to celebrate your accomplishments, so we thought we would help you today."*

"You can open it now or after you eat. It's up to you," Qadeer told her, motioning towards the present.

Yasmine smiled and broke into the paper. *"But open the card first,"* Lina reminded her. Yasmine set down the package and pulled off the card. It included a quote from the Qur'aan and a short poem in Arabic. Yasmine slowly read the words to herself before reading it aloud to her parents. The card also contained a bookmark with a cat curled up on it under the words *'Reading is Purrfect'*. Then she turned her attention back to the package.

Inside was a plain cardboard box. It was taped shut and she picked at the tape with her nails. When it wouldn't come off, Qadeer slipped a table knife under the tape to cut it. Yasmine lifted the lid and moved aside the tissue paper used to wrap her gift. She peered inside and then gasped. Carefully, she cupped the item in her hands and lifted it out. It was a beautiful *hijaab*. It was covered in detailed design and bluish colors. On the top was a beautiful flower made of what appeared to be jade or a similar stone. Yasmine rubbed her finger over it and felt the cool smoothness of the stone. Looking up at Lina and Qadeer, she said softly, *"Thank you! It's beautiful!"*

Both Qadeer and Lina smiled back. Qadeer said, *"You know Mr. Qais who owns the jewelry store? Well, I was there a few weeks ago and saw that in his display case. Apparently, it came from Jordan. I knew it was just perfect for my little Yasmine. I hope you will wear it this Eid, insha'Allaah."*

Yasmine got up and hugged her dad tightly before giving her mom a kiss. *"Thank you both! I will treasure it always!"*

Lina got up to remove the discarded wrapping paper from the table. *"Well, let's eat before breakfast gets cold."* She sat back down and started pouring juice into three cups.

Qadeer and Lina had been right about Yasmine's business. She had been so wrapped up in her work that she hadn't taken the time to acknowledge how much she had earned and how far she had come.

On Wednesday night, Yasmine carefully counted out the money in her fun jar. Other than the occasional book, she had not spent much on herself. In addition, she had far exceeded her $20 per week goal that was laid out in her business plan. Not only was she still doing chores around the house, but she was also helping some of the neighbors with their chores as well. That meant that she did have some expenses since she had to purchase cleaning supplies to take with her, but she had managed to make a tidy profit.

Pulling out the bills, she smoothed them out and split them into piles for each bill. Deciding that it would give her more room in the crowded jar, she counted out 20 $1 bills. Then she found an envelope from the desk and placed them inside. Taking the envelope to her backpack, she unzipped an inside pocket; she didn't want to lose the money on the way to school.

The next morning, she slipped quickly into the office and hoped that Sydney would not spot her. Putting down her backpack, she unzipped the bag and then the inner pocket. As she pulled out the envelope, Mrs. Newman looked up. *"How can I help you today, honey?"*

"I'd like the pink sweatshirt, please," Yasmine said, nodding in the direction of the Spirit Store display.

Mrs. Newman took the envelope and stood up. *"So, I see you've changed your mind about just having the t-shirt."*

"No, the sweatshirt isn't for me." Mrs. Newman looked around at Yasmine. *"It's for Sydney."*

"Well, aren't you a good friend! Sydney will be so happy..." She opened the cabinet where the sweatshirts were stored and rifled through them. *"Hmmmm...,"* she said, more to herself than Yasmine, *"what size for Sydney..."* Finally, she turned back to Yasmine. *"Sydney's something of a peanut so we'd better stick with the small."* She counted the money in the envelope and handed the sweatshirt over. Yasmine hustled out the door before Mrs. Newman could say good-bye.

In the kindergarten room, Mr. Jackson was seated behind his desk. *"Hi, Yasmine. This is a surprise...,"* he started to say, but Yasmine put her finger to her lips to signal his silence.

"It's a surprise," she whispered, as she hurried to the table where Sydney sat.

She set down the sweatshirt and pulled a piece of construction out of her backpack. It was a card that she had made the week before. It was pink, of course. Yasmine may have been smart and talented in some areas, but she was no artist. It simply said *'For You',* inside the card. She hoped Sydney would be surprised and would have no idea who it was from.

Before heading out the door, Yasmine turned to Mr. Jackson. *"Don't tell her, okay? I don't want her to know it's from me."* But before Mr. Jackson could reply, Yasmine was already out the door and down the hall.

At lunch, Yasmine was already seated when Sydney arrived. She was easy to spot with her bright pink sweatshirt. She made a beeline right to Yasmine and practically knocked her off her seat.

Her arms wrapped tightly around Yasmine's neck as she repeated, *"Thank you, thank you, thank you."*

Yasmine grasped Sydney's hands and tried to detach herself from the first grader. *"What?"* she tried unconvincingly to sound confused.

"Don't say what! You know what!" Sydney stepped back and pulled on the sweatshirt.

"Oh, you finally bought the sweatshirt," said Yasmine, still trying to look innocent, but the look on Sydney's face told her that there was no use trying to deny it. *"You weren't supposed to know!"* Yasmine sighed. *"Did Mr. Jackson tell you?"*

Sydney shook her head. *"No, I just knew. Who else would buy me a sweatshirt? And you're the only person who draws cougars that look like horses."* She smiled adoringly at Yasmine and then frowned. *"But I feel bad that you spent all this money on me. That's a lot of money, Yasmine."*

"Don't feel bad," said Yasmine. *"You'll make me feel bad if you feel bad."* She touched her friend's shoulder. Sydney's smile returned.

"Okay, I'm going to get lunch, and I'll be right back." As Yasmine's friend ran off to the lunch line, she sat feeling very good that she had made Sydney so very happy.

'Allaah will deprive usury of all blessing, but will give increase for deeds of charity.'

(The Qur'aan: Chapter 2, Verse 276)

It seemed appropriate to Yasmine that this should be the verse she was currently memorizing. After repeating it to her mother, she said, *"I gave the sweatshirt to Sydney today."*

"And how did she like it?"

"Oh, she was thrilled. I made a card, but didn't sign my name. I was hoping she wouldn't know it was from me, but she did."

"Well, good friends usually know what is on the other's mind," Lina stated.

Yasmine considered this, *"Or Mr. Jackson could have told her."*

"Even though she knew, it was a wonderful thing for you to do, Yasmine. Alhamdulillaah, you have a heart of gold." Lina took Yasmine's hand and squeezed it.

Yasmine plopped down on the couch beside her mom. She randomly picked up a book sitting on the end table next to her and looked at it. It was one of a series of books about a girl who ran a pet hotel. Yasmine had read the entire series and even gone over some of the books twice.

She looked over at her mom, *"Can we go to the library this weekend?"*

"I suppose," Lina said absently.

"I've already read this book twice and want to find something new."

Lina looked over at Yasmine, *"What about all the books in your room?"*

"Read them all."

"Really?"

Yasmine nodded.

"Hmmmm…," was all Lina could reply.

There was silence for a minute and then Yasmine asked, *"Do you think I could write a book, Mom?"*

Lina was about to say that she thought Yasmine was far too young to write a book but she stopped herself; *astaghfirUllaah*, Lina thought to herself. She should never doubt the good that Allaah could do through even a child. So instead, she said, *"It might be a challenge, but I don't see why not. What would you write about?"*

Yasmine continued to stare at the cover of the book she was holding. *"I don't know. Maybe a bird catcher who chases down lost birds?"* she said laughing.

Lina smiled at Yasmine's joke.

Her daughter continued, *"These books are fun to read, but if I wrote something I would want it to be about something more important. Something that would make Allaah pleased with of me,"* her voice trailed off.

"Well, there are other types of books not just fiction," Lina said as she brushed Yasmine's hair behind her ear. *"There are nonfiction books that tell people how to do things, and others make people aware of problems in the world and let them know what they can do to help."*

Yasmine considered this, *"So maybe a nonfiction book would be better. But what would I write about?"*

"Why don't we talk about that after dinner? You need to do your Arabic now. Run and get your stuff. I'll meet you at the table." Lina stood up and walked towards the kitchen.

Yasmine began to pull her papers out of the desk while still thinking about how she could best honor Allaah by writing a book. *Insha'Allaah*, she thought to herself. Please, Allaah, help me find the path that is best for me - *aameen*.

In what was becoming a regular habit, Yasmine and Lina met at the table that night after dinner. *"So let's talk about your idea for a book,"* Lina began.

"Well, I don't really have an idea yet. That's the problem…maybe it's a dumb idea," Yasmine shrugged.

"No! Don't say that!" Lina exclaimed. *"Insha'Allaah, this idea could be straight from Allaah! You do think that this idea comes from Allaah, right?"*

Yasmine nodded. *"But I'm only 7,"* she protested. *"What can Allaah do with me?"*

"We'll let Allaah judge that," Lina replied. She slipped a piece of paper and pencil in front of Yasmine. *"Let's start by figuring out what your heart is telling you to do."*

Yasmine took the pencil and at Lina's prompting began to write down all the things that interested her. When she was finished, she had written:

I like cats, helping people, my family, school, Sydney Mrs. Chrisman, Allaah, apple cider, cooking and writing.

"Okay, now let's think about these things," Lina suggested. *"Maybe you could write something about cats? You love them so much; you could share that love with others."*

Yasmine considered this for a minute. Her mom was right that she loved cats; something about their warm, fuzzy bodies and soft purring just fascinated Yasmine. Although she was not the type of girl to constantly worry about what others had and she did not, Yasmine was desperate for a cat of her own. Still, writing about cats didn't seem to be what she wanted to do.

She shook her head slowly, *"No, Mom, I don't think that's it. I do love cats, but I really want to help people."* She stared at the list some more.

"Well," said Lina, *"how about a cookbook?"* Yasmine considered this for a moment. Lina continued, *"It could be a kids' cookbook."*

Again, she slowly shook her head. Yasmine said, *"Cooking is fun, but it just doesn't feel right. I want to help people who really need help. I mean, it's good to have fun cooking, but it doesn't help people who really need help. Do you know what I mean?"* she looked at her mom questioningly.

"Yes, I know what you mean, honey," Lina assured her. *"So who do you want to help? Kids or adults?"*

"Everyone," Yasmine replied quickly.

Lina paused. There were so many different ways to help people. She didn't know what question to ask next to help Yasmine. She said a silent prayer in the hopes that Allaah would give her the wisdom she needed. Then she looked up at Yasmine and said, *"Let's make a list of all the different problems that people face today."*

Yasmine picked up her pencil again and began writing all the problems she knew:

People without food
Children without parents
Alcohol and drug use
People without homes
Divorce
Smoking
Lying and stealing
People don't believe in God
Wars

When she was done, Lina looked over the list and sighed, *"A lot of problems in the world aren't there?"* Yasmine frowned in response. *"So which of these speaks to you, my dear?"*

Looking at the list, Yasmine prayed silently in her heart. Then she looked around her. The weather was still cool, and the furnace was humming quietly in the background. In the living room she could see her father sitting on the overstuffed couch looking over some work papers. She closed her eyes and thought of her warm bed upstairs that would be waiting for her after her final prayers.

She looked at the list again. Some people don't have all this. Yasmine had heard about some people who lived under bridges or in cars or in cots at shelters where they would have to pack up and leave in the morning. Yasmine tried to imagine what it would be like to go with her mom and dad to a shelter. To have everything she owned in a backpack. A tear welled in the corner of her eye, and she shook the thought from her mind.

"I want to help people who don't have homes," she said, looking up at her mom. The tear slipped down the side of her cheek. *"Everyone should have their own bed."*

Lina nodded and leaned over to kiss her daughter. *"How right you are, how right you are. Insha'Allaah, you will write a book to help those who are homeless."*

On Saturday, Yasmine and Lina visited the local library. The librarian showed Yasmine how to use the computer catalog system to locate books on homelessness. Lina was amazed to think that when she was a child searching for books was a long process of flipping through the card catalog. Now, within a matter of seconds, Yasmine had narrowed her search to a hundred or so books on the subject.

The librarian walked with Yasmine to the bookshelves and showed her how to search by number for the books she wanted. When Yasmine wanted a book that wasn't available at the local library, the librarian ordered it from a library in the next town over. After an hour of intense searching, Yasmine and Lina left the library with a bag full of books and promises that more would be arriving shortly through the interlibrary loan program.

At home, Yasmine headed straight to her room. She separated out the books into stacks. She had found several fiction books that were written for children on the subject of homelessness, and she placed those in one stack. Then, the fiction books were separated into piles depending on their reading level. Yasmine decided that she would start with the thinnest books first before moving on to the more difficult books.

Once the books were sorted, Yasmine sat on her bed with a pencil and notebook by her side. She took the first book off the stack and opened it up to begin reading. As she read, she wrote down notes and ideas for her book as she thought of them. By the time it was *Dhuhr salaah*, Yasmine had worked halfway through the first stack of books.

In the evening, as she prayed with her family, Yasmine could not help but feel a special appreciation for all Allaah had blessed her with. She looked lovingly at her mother and father and then thought to herself of all the times she had been ungrateful; of all the times when she had felt angry at her parents, or even Allaah, if things did not go her way.

As she lay in bed that night, the last thought on Yasmine's mind was that she would never take her life for granted again; *astaghfirUllaah*.

Chapter 4

A New Obstacle To Face

Although it was still August, Yasmine was up well before dawn. She yawned deeply and stretched as she got out of bed. Normally, she had to wake up for *Fajr* prayer but then she hopped back into bed afterwards. But Yasmine's family had entered the month of Ramadan so there were no more late mornings of sleep for her.

She joined her mom and dad at the table for breakfast. They would eat the early meal before praying Fajr, and then spend the day fasting as a way to reflect upon and worship Allaah (SWT). By the time their morning ritual was over, Yasmine was much too awake to think about going back to bed.

When she was younger Ramadan was a difficult time for Yasmine. This was especially true when she started school. Yasmine was one of few Muslims in the area, and none of her classmates understood why she wouldn't eat during the day. Even though kids are not required to fast Yasmine had tried for several days to do it when she was 6 years old.

In the past Ramadan was just a month that must be endured. But now that she was older, Yasmine sensed the deeper significance of the prayers and the fasting. As the ninth month of the Islamic calendar, Ramadan remembers the time in which the Qur'aan was revealed to the Prophet Muhammad (SAAW), and is one of the five pillars of Islam.

As she continued her work on her book about homelessness, she was especially aware of how important it was to thank Allaah for the gift of the Qur'aan and all His other blessings as well.

During this month, the family also made visits to their local mosque every evening to hear the Qur'aan being recited.

One evening, as Yasmine practiced her Arabic, she looked up at her mom who was preparing dinner. *"Why do you wear a head scarf when you go out, Mom?"* she asked.

Lina was startled by the interruption. She touched her neck, *"Oh, this? Why it's my hijaab. Allaah (SWT) tells us in the Qur'aan that we must always dress modestly. For women, this means that we must cover ourselves and preserve our beauty; our beauty is only for our husbands and immediate family."*

"Why don't I wear a hijaab?" Yasmine asked.

"Well, insha'Allaah you will when you become older; but you are a child right now, and children are not bound by the same rules of dress," Lina explained. *"Of course, you must always be modest.*

That is why you must wear long shirts and pants. Shorts and tank tops might give people attention from others, but they do not please Allaah."

Yasmine listened carefully and then asked, *"Can I wear a hijaab if I want?"*

"Of course, you can," Lina answered.

"Okay, I want to," Yasmine said.

Lina smiled. *"We'll have to go shopping later tonight. I normally buy my clothes over the internet since most of the stores here don't sell the type of clothes I like."* She gestured to her outfit. *"I prefer to wear a jilbaab – a long tunic or dress - with loose pants underneath. But almost everything in the stores is too tight or too short."*

"I'd like to have some clothes like you too," Yasmine said. *"I think you look beautiful."*

"You are very kind, and I would certainly love to help you pick out some clothes." Lina added, *"But you must be prepared. Not many people wear a hijaab. Some people might stare at you or even laugh. Do you understand that?"*

Yasmine nodded and went back to her Arabic. Lina turned back to the counter and felt conflicted. She loved that Yasmine wanted to wear the *hijaab*, but she also wondered what sort of trouble she would encounter at school. Thinking back to when she first started wearing the *hijaab*, Lina remembered the teasing she had encountered from people she thought were her friends. She prayed that Yasmine would not have to endure the same thing.

When the first day of school rolled around, Yasmine appeared for breakfast wearing her Maple Valley t-shirt. Lina did a double-take at her daughter's appearance. Yasmine had been regularly wearing a *hijaab* and *jilbaab* at home for the last few weeks. She had even ventured out to the library and the store wearing her new clothes; but now that school was starting, it appeared that her courage had left her.

Yasmine seemed to notice her mother's reaction. *"I just wanted to wear my school shirt for the first day of school,"* she said apologetically. She quickly added, *"I'll wear my hijaab another day...just not the first day of school."*

Lina turned back to Yasmine, *"It is fine, my love. You are not bound to wear the hijaab, and if you want to wear your old clothes, that is fine."*

"You're not mad?"

Lina laughed lightly, *"Mad? Absolutely not! Remember, I was once a little girl too. I know how hard it can be to do something that your friends are not doing."* She gave Yasmine an encouraging kiss. *"I am pleased that you are wearing your hijaab at home and am sure that you will start wearing it to school as soon as you are ready."*

Yasmine was relieved. She had sat in her room for quite some time this morning staring at her *hijaab*. She wanted to wear it, she really did; but she was already nervous about the first day of school, and she didn't want to wear something that would make her even more nervous. *AstaghfirUllaah*, she hoped Allaah (SWT) would understand.

Getting off the bus, Yasmine clung to her backpack. She couldn't remember being this nervous last year, but here she was almost shaking. Over the summer, the school had sent a letter saying that Yasmine would be in Mrs. Richland's second grade class this year. Maybe that is what made Yasmine nervous. While Mrs. Chrisman was always smiling and listening, Mrs. Richland always seemed annoyed.

In the hallway, someone grabbed the back of Yasmine's shirt. She swung around to see Sydney there. Sydney minus her long curls. Her younger friend beamed up at her, *"Hi, Yasmine!"*

Yasmine smiled in relief to see a friendly face, *"Hi, Sydney! What happened to your hair?"*

Sydney shyly touched her short new haircut, *"I cut it off. It was so hot in the summer."*

Yasmine giggled too, *"Yeah, it was hot this summer!"* Sydney shrugged. *"Who's your teacher this year?"* Yasmine asked.

"Mrs. Chrisman!"

"Lucky you! I have Mrs. Richland," Yasmine shared.

"Oh," Sydney said, her face falling. *"My mom says that she is a firm teacher."*

The bell rang, and the two girls gave each other a quick hug and promised to meet again at lunch.

Down the hall was Mrs. Richland's room. Inside, Yasmine saw several familiar faces, including Grace and Tom. There were also some kids she recognized from other classes last year; Ben and Tammy had both been in Mr. Riley's first grade classroom last year. Then there were a few kids that Yasmine had never seen before; she wasn't sure if they were new to the school or if she simply didn't recognize them from the year before.

By the desk, Mrs. Richland was greeting students and directing them to their desks. She was smiling, and Yasmine suddenly felt that she had misjudged her teacher. But then as Mrs. Richland saw Yasmine approach, her smile disappeared. *"Hello, Yasmine. Your desk is right there,"* Mrs. Richland pointed to the seat next to Grace.

Yasmine took her seat and said hi to Grace, who seemed to ignore her. Grace and Yasmine had been friends in kindergarten, but last year Grace apparently decided that she was cool and Yasmine was not. They stopped spending time together by the middle of first grade.

Mrs. Richland walked to the front of the room and clapped her hands together, *"All right, children, time to begin. Quiet down please."*

The students who remained standing all shuffled to their seats, and the room quickly came to order. Once everyone was seated, Mrs. Richland continued, *"Now children, I know some of you are old friends from last year, and I know some of you are new this year. So let's start by telling one another something about what we enjoy doing. Let's share what we did on Sunday."*

Even though Yasmine was not in the front row, Mrs. Richland stared directly at her. *"Why don't you start, Yasmine? What did you do on Sunday after church?"*

Caught off-guard by the question, Yasmine could only say, *"Church?"*

"Yes, Yasmine, church. On Sunday after church, what did your family do?"

"We don't go to church…," Yasmine stammered.

Mrs. Richland did not look at all surprised by this answer, but asked anyway, *"Whatever do you mean, Yasmine?"*

Yasmine was flustered but managed to say, *"We don't go to church but we go to the mosque most nights to read the Qur'aan."*

With feigned innocence, Mrs. Richland raised her eyebrows and said, *"Really?"*

"Mrs. Richland, Yasmine doesn't believe in God. She's a Muslim," Grace said airily.

A warm flush crept up Yasmine's neck and face. Grace was wrong, but she was so embarrassed; Yasmine couldn't think of anything to say. She sat there blushing fiercely as Grace snickered and the rest of the class stared.

"Hmmmm…pity," Mrs. Richland said. *"Well, nothing we can do about that I suppose. Grace, why don't you tell us about your Sunday."*

Grace launched into a long explanation of the Sunday sermon and how her family had then gone to the park for a church potluck. As Grace talked Yasmine fought back tears. She had never been more embarrassed in her life. She silently prayed that the floor would open up and swallow her desk whole so she could disappear from the room.

At lunch, Yasmine waited, dejected at the lunch table. Since it was still Ramadan, she would not eat until after evening prayers. Sitting alone with no lunch in front of her, Grace walked by and said something Yasmine couldn't quite make out. But Grace and all her friends started laughing, and Yasmine could only imagine that they were talking about her.

Sydney bounded up to the table as her normal perky self. She plopped down next to Yasmine and started talking at breakneck speed about her day. It wasn't until she had gone halfway through describing her morning that she realized Yasmine wasn't paying attention. *"What's wrong?"* she said.

Yasmine related her experience in class that morning as tears slid down her cheeks. *"Oh, Yasmine. I'm so sorry!"* Sydney squeezed her friend's shoulder and then turned back to her food. She couldn't think of what else to say to make her feel better. *"Should we put tacks on Mrs. Richland's chair? Or throw food at Grace as she walks by?"* Yasmine only shook her head.

Realizing that she was not eating, Sydney asked, *"Did you already eat?"* Yasmine shook her head again. *"Do you want one of my cookies?"* Sydney held one out, *"My mom made them last night."* Yasmine shook her head again.

Out of ideas to make Yasmine feel better, the two girls sat in silence for the remainder of lunch.

On the bus ride home, Yasmine decided not to say anything to her parents. She didn't want to upset them; and as much as she disliked her, she didn't want to get Mrs. Richland in trouble either.

"Assalaamu-alaykum, dear, how was the first day of school?" Lina greeted Yasmine at the door.

Yasmine put on her best smile and said, *"It was okay."*

"It doesn't look like it was okay," Lina observed.

"It's just that Mrs. Richland isn't as nice as Mrs. Chrisman. That's all. And all my friends are in different rooms this year," Yasmine explained.

Lina hugged her, *"Give it time, honey. It will get better, I am sure."* Yasmine hugged her mom back, but she wasn't so sure that it would get better.

Everyday at school Yasmine kept herself to herself. Other than lunch and recess which she spent with Sydney, she didn't talk to anyone. In the classroom, Yasmine avoided Mrs. Richland's gaze and was careful to keep her eyes on her paperwork. She knew Grace and some of the other kids talked about her but she ignored them. *Allaahu Akbar, Allaahu Akbar, Allaahu Akbar,* she kept this prayer ever in her mind. She was certain that Allaah would get her through this trial just as He had done for His people so many times in the past.

'O children of Adam, we have provided you with garments to cover your bodies, as well as for luxury. But the best garment is the garment of righteousness.'

(The Qur'aan; Chapter 7, Verse 26)

This was the verse Yasmine was currently studying. She pondered it deeply each night before she went to bed. *AstaghfirUllaah*, she prayed. She felt so small and weak for not being able to stand up for her beliefs. Mrs. Richland had made a regular habit of commenting on church matters and her personal belief. Yasmine was sure that it was not appropriate for Mrs. Richland to be saying such things in school, but she wasn't sure what to do. And since it didn't seem to upset anyone else Yasmine kept her thoughts to herself.

Still, there was this nagging feeling deep in Yasmine that she should not just be sitting idly; that she should be doing something to show others that she believed in Allaah and that Allaah is 'God'. But between these feelings was also the nervousness of being different. She didn't want to draw attention to herself. She didn't want to be the one that the other kids stared at and Mrs. Richland picked on. Sleep didn't come easy that night. She tossed and turned, trying to figure out what to do.

In the morning, Yasmine appeared for breakfast wearing her *hijaab* and *jilbaab*. Qadeer said as she entered, *"Here is our young lady."*

Lina turned around and smiled, *"Yasmine! You are wearing your hijaab today!"* Yasmine smiled at her mother. *"Are you sure?"* Lina asked.

"Yes," said Yasmine. *"I am sure. I don't want to hide who I am."* But inside, Yasmine's stomach was turning to knots. She barely touched her breakfast and prayed for strength during the *Fajr* prayer. On the bus ride she kept her face firmly planted towards the window and pretended to be completely absorbed in what was outside. She avoided the gaze of the students even though she knew they were all looking at here. Pulling up to the school, her biggest fear was how Sydney and Mrs. Chrisman would react. These were the two people who made school bearable. She didn't know what she would do if they stopped talking to her.

In the hallway Yasmine hurried to her room with her head down. She wasn't sure what to do. She didn't want to go in the room with Mrs. Richland, but she didn't want to stand in the hall with the other students either. She spotted Sydney down the hall and debated whether to go to her. Instead, she took a quick turn and headed into a different classroom.

Mrs. Chrisman was bending over her desk organizing some papers. *"Hi,"* Yasmine said in a quiet voice.

Looking up, Mrs. Chrisman's signature smile spread across her face and a wave of relief washed over Yasmine. *"Hello, Yasmine. Don't you look pretty today!"* With twinkling eyes, Mrs. Chrisman walked to Yasmine and touched her *jilbaab*. *"Is this new?"*

"Not brand new. My mom bought it a month ago," Yasmine explained. *"But today is the first day I am wearing it to school."*

"Well, it looks lovely on you." Mrs. Chrisman looked towards the door where several students were entering.

Sydney came in behind the group and stopped when she saw Yasmine. Her eyes clouded for a moment and then she said, *"Yasmine?"*

Yasmine's fear came rushing back. Sydney didn't like the *hijaab*. Yasmine was losing a friend.

"Of course it's Yasmine, Sydney," Mrs. Chrisman said. *"Isn't her new outfit fabulous?"*

Sydney shook her head for a minute as if in a daze and then smiled. *"Absolutely!"* She rushed over for a closer look. *"I didn't recognize you for a minute. I'm so used to looking for your long hair."* This was followed with a flurry of questions about Yasmine's new look and where she got her clothes.

The classroom was quickly filling now, and Mrs. Chrisman glanced at the clock, *"You'd better run to your room, Yasmine. School is about to start."*

Feeling much more confident, Yasmine ran down the hall. She sprinted into her room and hung up her backpack. She had almost forgotten that she was dressed differently until she realized that everyone was staring at her. Putting her head down, she quickly hurried to her desk and sat down.

The bell rang, and Mrs. Richland walked to the front of the room. *"Take it off, Yasmine,"* she said briskly.

"What?" Yasmine looked up confused.

"Hats are not allowed in school. Take it off!" Mrs. Richland said sternly.

"It's not a hat; it's a hijaab."

"I don't care what you call it; it's not allowed in school," Mrs. Richland retorted.

For a moment, Yasmine's hands moved to her head. She started to pull the *hijaab* back and then thought better of it, *"No, Mrs. Richland. My mom and dad said I could wear it to school."*

Mrs. Richland let out something that sounded like a grunt. She was obviously surprised to hear a student talk back to her. *"Oh no, not in my classroom you won't."* She stomped towards Yasmine who cowered in her seat. Grabbing the *hijaab*, Mrs. Richland yanked it off her head. Yasmine let out a scream as some of her hair went with it.

"And don't let me ever catch you coming to school with this again. And you'd better not ever talk back to me, young lady. Do you understand me?" Mrs. Richland was hovering over Yasmine. When she didn't reply, Mrs. Richland said again, even louder, *"Do you understand me?!"*

Yasmine nodded meekly and stared at her desk. Please, please Allaah she thought...please don't let me cry in front of everyone. Mrs. Richland huffed back to her desk and threw the *hijaab* in a drawer. Grace laughed quietly. Yasmine sank into her desk and once again wished that she could simply disappear.

By lunchtime, most of the school had heard the story. It seemed as though everyone stared at Yasmine as she walked by. The laughter and snickering were almost too much to bear. Sydney tried her best to console Yasmine at lunch, but it was no use. Yasmine was contemplating just running away and hiding in the library until school was out but decided that it would only draw more attention to her.

That afternoon, she could not control the flood of tears when she got home. After sharing what had happened with her *hijaab* in school, Yasmine told her mother all about the first day of school and Mrs. Richland's many other comments. Lina was distraught herself but tried to comfort her daughter. She felt awful that Yasmine had to endure such trials.

Rather than working on her Islamic studies, Lina sent Yasmine upstairs when Qadeer came home. Yasmine absently flipped through her notes for her book on homelessness and flipped through a book or two. She could hear her parents in deep discussion downstairs. Shortly, Qadeer called her down.

Lina looked with deep concern at her daughter, *"I am so sorry that this happened, Yasmine. Your father is going to take you to school tomorrow and talk to the principal."*

Yasmine nodded, *"Is Mrs. Richland going to get into trouble?"*

Qadeer snorted, *"Trouble! She should be fired!"*

"We don't know what will happen," Lina said, *"but we hope that we can at least get you transferred to a different room. And Mrs. Richland should be set straight about her beliefs about Muslims. Unfortunately, there are a lot of misconceptions about our faith. She obviously believes those and not the truth."*

"Should I get out my Arabic papers now?" Yasmine asked.

"Why don't you take the night off," Qadeer suggested, *"you could do with a break."*

Yasmine agreed, *"I could go work on my book instead."*

"Okay," said Lina, *"but I want you to know how very proud I am for the way you acted today. It took a lot of courage to stand up for your beliefs that way."*

Wiping her tear-streaked cheeks, Yasmine felt slightly better. It had been an awful experience, but at least she had been true to

Allaah (SWT) and what He would have wanted. She turned to walk back upstairs.

"*Yasmine,*" her father stopped her, "*we love you very much.*"

Smiling for the first time that night, Yasmine reminded herself how blessed she was to have wonderful parents.

The next day, Yasmine again came down for breakfast wearing a *hijaab*. "*Oh, Yasmine, are you sure?*" Lina asked. Yasmine nodded. She had decided last night that she wasn't going to let Mrs. Richland bully her.

After breakfast and prayer, Yasmine spent some time re-arranging her book notes. Since her father was taking her to school, she didn't need to leave so early. She had been working on the book for almost 5 months. She had several notebooks worth of notes and loose papers that she had photocopied. In her mind, she had a rough outline of how she wanted the book to read. Her special prayer during Ramadan was that Allaah (SWT) would give her wisdom on how best to organize the book.

When it was time to go to school, Qadeer buckled up next to Yasmine and looked stern, "*We will clear this up. No one treats my daughter that way.*"

At school, Qadeer and Yasmine walked directly to the office. Mrs. Newman looked startled to see Qadeer. He was an imposing man and at this moment he did not appear happy. "*I must speak to the principal at once.*"

Mrs. Newman nodded, "*Mr. Kelly is in his office. Let me see if he is available.*" She left for a moment and then returned. "*You can go right in,*" she said, gesturing to an open door.

Qadeer turned to Yasmine, "*You must wait here.*" He then entered the door and shut it behind him. Yasmine sat on one of the chairs in the office, staring at her hands in her lap.

There was a large frosted window on the Principal's office. Yasmine looked up occasionally and could see her father and the principal talking. After a few minutes, Mr. Kelly emerged from the office, "*Mrs. Newman, can you send someone down to cover Mrs. Richland's room. Tell her to come here immediately.*" Mrs. Newman nodded and summoned another secretary who left for Mrs. Richland's room.

Several minutes later, Mrs. Richland entered. She glared at Yasmine as she walked by. Mrs. Newman stood and escorted her to Mr. Kelly's office. Inside, Yasmine could see her father stand when Mrs. Richland entered. He began to talk loudly, and Mr. Kelly gestured for him to calm down. Then, the principal talked at length with Qadeer adding comments occasionally. Mrs. Richland left the office and again glared at Yasmine as she walked by.

Then, Mr. Kelly and Qadeer exited the room. Mr. Kelly spoke to Yasmine, *"I am very sorry, Yasmine. I had no idea that Mrs. Richland was treating you like that. And there is no excuse for her behavior yesterday. I've spoken to Mrs. Richland, but I think it will be best if we move you to Mrs. Mitchell's room instead."*

Yasmine did not know Mrs. Mitchell. She was a new teacher this year. Mr. Kelly must have seen the hesitation in her eyes for he added, *"Let me tell you about Mrs. Mitchell. She recently moved from the State, and I understand she has a cousin who is Muslim. So I think you will find her very understanding."*

With a brief smile, Mr. Kelly whisked Yasmine down the hall to Mrs. Mitchell's room. He called Mrs. Mitchell to the door and spoke with her briefly. Mrs. Mitchell glanced at Yasmine and smiled when their eyes met. The new teacher held out a hand to Yasmine, *"We would love to have you join us."*

Mrs. Mitchell's smile put Yasmine's heart somewhat at ease. She looked back at Qadeer who nodded for her to go to the classroom. Yasmine walked forward, and Mrs. Mitchell put her hand around her shoulder. The other students were working at their desks and Mrs. Mitchell pointed to an empty desk in the corner, *"Why don't you have a seat there, and I will be with you in a moment. We'll also get all your stuff shortly."*

Yasmine took a seat, and Mrs. Mitchell spoke briefly with Qadeer. Then she walked back to Yasmine to discuss the daily routine.

At lunch, Yasmine felt better than she had all school year. Mrs. Mitchell had been very nice, just as promised. Realizing that she had not seen Sydney all day, she scanned the lunch crowd for her. As she searched, Sydney appeared by her side. On her head was a bright pink head scarf, *"Like it?"* she said with a flourish.

Yasmine giggled, *"Why are you wearing a headscarf?"*

"Because I hear all the really cool kids wear one," Sydney said smiling. Then she turned serious, *"I just didn't want you to feel weird being the only one with a scarf. So my mom had this only scarf in her closet, and she showed me how to wrap it."*

It was no *hijaab*, but Yasmine was overcome with gratitude to her friend for thinking of her this way. She leaned over and hugged Sydney. *"Thank you,"* she whispered.

Chapter 5

Being Creative

This morning was different. After a month of getting up to cold cereal or toast before morning prayer (*Fajr*), Yasmine woke to the aroma of pancakes and eggs. Looking at her clock, she jumped out of bed in a hurry. If she hoped to eat before morning prayer (*Fajr*), she was late. Running down the stairs, she rushed to the table.

Lina looked up from her cooking and smiled, *"No need to hurry today Yasmine...it's Eid ul-Fitr!"*

"Oh!" Yasmine said in surprise. Ramadan was done. The period of fasting was over, and her family could feast today.

"We'll eat in just a moment and then head to the mosque, insh'Allaah," Lina explained.

Yasmine wandered into the living room to prepare for the *Fajr salaah*. Her father was unrolling his prayer mat. *"Eid Mubarak, my love,"* Qadeer said when he saw her.

After the morning prayer (*Fajr*), the family enjoyed Lina's breakfast before heading to the mosque. Yasmine changed into a new outfit bought specially for the Eid. At home, after the Eid prayer, gifts were given to Yasmine. Throughout the day, Yasmine felt a special sense of peace and belonging. *Allaahu Akbar*, God is Great.

Several days later, Qadeer asked Yasmine at dinner, *"How is your book coming? We haven't heard much about it lately?"*

Yasmine had been giving her parents almost nightly updates on the progress of her book. However, she had not worked lately on her project. *"Oh, I've been so focused on Ramadan that I haven't spent much time on the book,"* Yasmine answered.

"Oh," Qadeer said, *"because I was wondering if you were giving up on it."*

"No," said Yasmine. *"Actually, I've got almost all my notes organized. I think I am going to start writing tonight."*

"I have a better idea for tonight," Qadeer took a bite of food from his plate. After swallowing, he continued, *"There is a special tonight on the public television station about homelessness in America. I read about it in the paper. It might be a good program for you to watch...unless you want to write tonight instead?"*

"Oh no!" Yasmine exclaimed, *"That's a great idea, Dad!"*

Television was a special treat for Yasmine. The family rarely watched TV. They owned one set. It was actually stored in a closet. However, when there was a program of interest Qadeer would pull it out and set it up in the living room. Sometimes, on rainy days,

Lina would put in a video for Yasmine, but it was generally something to help with her Arabic or Islamic studies.

Yasmine really didn't mind not watching TV. In fact, she was so busy between school, studies, her cleaning business and her book, that she couldn't imagine having the time to just sit and watch television. It seemed so unproductive; but when her classmates were going on and on about the latest star or the newest show, Yasmine couldn't help but feel left out. Still, she understood the reason why television was limited. It sounded like some of her friends spent all night sitting in front of the television; and what they watched didn't sound like programs Allaah (SWT) would be pleased with.

After dinner, Qadeer pulled the television out of the closet. He pulled the coffee table back to the far wall and centered the set on the table. He plugged it and went back to the closet. After rummaging through a couple shelves, he found what he was looking for; he brought back the rabbit ear antenna and attached it to the television. Turning the television on, he swung the antenna until the signal came in relatively clear.

He looked at his watch, *"There, you're all set, Yasmine. The program starts in half an hour, so you have some free time."*

Yasmine thanked her dad and then bounded up the stairs to her room. In an old milk crate, she had stored all her notebooks and several folders full of pages. For almost 5 months, she had spent at least an hour each night poring over books and writing notes. At night, she dreamt of homelessness and often woke with a new idea of something to include in her book. She always kept a notebook on her nightstand so she could jot down her thoughts first thing before they left her.

Now she grabbed the entire crate and brought it downstairs. *"Oh my!"* Lina exclaimed when she saw Yasmine heave the crate onto a chair. She knew that Yasmine had been doing extensive research, but she had no idea that she had accumulated so much material.

Lina and Yasmine had made weekly visits to the library. The librarian knew Yasmine so well that she often set aside newspaper clippings and books that she thought Yasmine might be interested in. While Lina knew Yasmine was a determined child, she wasn't sure if the book idea would fizzle out. She continued to gently encourage her, but she also didn't want to push her daughter too hard. Lina had been glad that Qadeer brought up the matter at dinner since she too was curious if Yasmine had given up. Now, seeing the crate of research materials, there was no doubt in Lina's mind that Yasmine would see her book written.

When it was time for the program, Lina and Qadeer sat down with Yasmine. She sat on the edge of the couch with a notebook and pencil ready. Throughout the show, she scribbled notes. At the end, Lina and Qadeer discussed the program with Yasmine to make sure she had understood everything that was presented.

The following night, Yasmine began to write. She had already written the opening chapter a hundred times in her mind. Now, it was just a question of putting it on paper. With a fresh notebook, Yasmine spread out her notes on the kitchen table and sat down with pencil in hand. Her handwriting had not improved much since first grade, and her pace was painstakingly slow. She tried to write in her very best print so that the book would be easy to read. After 30 minutes, she had not even covered one sheet of paper. She stretched her hand and looked at her paper, frustrated.

"How's it coming along, honey?" Lina walked into the kitchen.

Yasmine sighed, *"It's going to take forever, Mom! At this rate the book will be done when I'm 21."*

Lina walked over to the table and looked over Yasmine's shoulder, *"What seems to be the problem?"*

Yasmine held up the paper, *"This is the problem. It took me half an hour to write this, and I have all this to cover,"* Yasmine gestured to the stacks of notes on the table. She collapsed onto the table and threw her face into her arms.

Rubbing her back, Lina thought for a moment, *"Do you know how to type on the computer?"*

"We have computer class at school so we do a little typing."

"Well, let's try that then," Lina suggested. *"Grab your notebook and come with me."*

The computer was located in a den that Qadeer used for work. Yasmine didn't come in the room often since her father needed to work uninterrupted. Walking in, Yasmine breathed deeply the smell of clean, polished wood and the slightly musty smell of old books. Qadeer's den also housed an impression personal library with his most treasured book being an old copy of the Qur'aan that had been passed down through his family.

Lina started up the computer and opened a word processing program. *"Okay, let's see how this goes. It is all ready for you to start typing. I'll be back to check on you shortly."*

Half an hour later, Lina returned to the den. Yasmine looked up at her mom. *"It's no use,"* Yasmine said, fighting back tears, *"I can't type fast either."*

Lina walked around the desk and looked at the screen. Sure enough, Yasmine had not even gotten through what she had written in half an hour. *"Hmmmm...,"* she thought.

Tears coursing down her cheeks now, Yasmine allowed herself to cry. *"It'll never happen, Mom. I can't write my book. All this research was for nothing,"* she leaned back in the oversized office chair and sobbed.

"No, no, don't say that," Lina comforted her, *"insha'Allaah, Allaah (SWT) will show us a way. We just need to think about this problem and put our trust in Him."*

It wasn't until a week later that the answer presented itself. As she often did, Yasmine stepped into Mrs. Chrisman's classroom to visit her and Sydney before the start of the school day. Although Yasmine liked Mrs. Mitchell, she always felt totally at ease in Mrs. Chrisman's classroom.

On this day, Sydney had not yet arrived. Mrs. Chrisman was helping one of her students with a homework assignment so Yasmine waited near the door for a minute. She didn't have anything important to say to Mrs. Chrisman, but she didn't want to go to her class yet. Instead, she pretended to be fascinated by the bulletin board in the room. It was covered with large paper teeth. Each tooth was labeled with a month, and inside each one was listed the names of students who lost teeth that month.

When Mrs. Chrisman was finished with her student, she smiled at Yasmine. *"How are you doing today?"* she asked.

Yasmine shrugged. She had felt out of sorts since her difficulty writing her book. She continued to write each night, but it was at a snail's pace. It was so frustrating to have these great ideas in her head and no way to get them out.

"It looks like something is on your mind," Mrs. Chrisman observed.

Yasmine nodded, *"I'm having trouble with my book."*

"Oh, what sort of trouble? Do you have writer's block?"

"No, I know exactly what I want to say, but I can't write or type fast enough to get it on paper. It's going to take forever."

"That is a problem," Mrs. Chrisman agreed, *"but I think I might have a solution."*

Yasmine's face brightened instantly, *"Really?"*

Mrs. Chrisman nodded, *"Yup, I think I know what will work."* She explained, *"They make special software just for people who can't type well. We use it at school for some of our students who need extra help."* Yasmine was all ears as Mrs. Chrisman continued, *"It lets you speak into a microphone and the program turns it into words on the computer."*

"So, I don't type the words, I just speak them?" Yasmine asked.

"That's right," Mrs. Chrisman smiled. *"Of course, it's not perfect. Sometimes it doesn't hear you right, and you need to double-check the punctuation and grammar, but it's a lot faster than writing by hand. Depending on the version you get, it costs about $50-$75, so it isn't cheap."*

"Oh, I've got at least that much in my fun jar at home." Yasmine was giddy thinking about how quickly she could get through her book now.

The bell rang, and Yasmine thanked Mrs. Chrisman for the tenth time. Then she ran down to her classroom, her mind swimming with happiness. She couldn't wait to get home that day.

The bus had barely stopped before Yasmine was up and running down the aisle. *"Yasmine, wait 'till we stop please,"* the bus driver reminded her.

"Sorry," Yasmine said breathlessly as she jumped from the top step to the ground. Winter was quickly approaching, and snow flurries filled the air. At top speed, she sprinted down the street to her home.

Slamming the door behind her, Yasmine yelled out, *"Mom! Mom! Where are you, Mom?"*

Lina walked out of the kitchen looking cross, *"There is no reason to shout, Yasmine. I am right here. And we do not slam the door like that."*

"Sorry, Mom, but Allaah (SWT) sent me the answer!"

After dinner, Yasmine emptied her fun jar out onto the table. Even while researching her book she had continued her cleaning business. Although she didn't do as much work as she used to, she had earned a significant amount of money. Her savings and Hajj jars were also stuffed full. The charity jar was emptied weekly to be donated. Since starting to work on her book, Yasmine's favorite place to send her *sadaqah* was the local homeless shelter.

Spreading out the bills and coins, Yasmine counted out $75. *"Mrs. Chrisman said that the most expensive version is $75 so I'll take out that much,"* Yasmine explained to her mother.

"You'll need some extra for tax," Lina stated.

"What's tax?" Yasmine asked.

Lina sat down at the table, *"Tax is money we pay to the government so that they can provide things like the roads, police and schools. Your father and I pay income taxes each year to both the federal and state governments and then the state adds a sales tax to each purchase you make in a store."*

"What is the federal government?"

"The federal government is in charge of all the United States. And then each state has their own government to make specific laws for that state."

Yasmine considered this, *"So the state adds a tax to everything we buy?"*

Lina nodded.

"But I didn't pay a tax at the Spirit Store."

"Well, tax can be hard to understand, especially for children. So I would guess that the school already figured the price of the tax into the items they sell. That way they don't have any sad students who didn't bring enough money to cover the tax."

"Oh," Yasmine said.

Lina looked at the remaining money on the table. Even after pulling out the $75 there was quite a bit left. *"We should probably think about getting you a bank account."*

"Why?" Yasmine asked.

"Because you have a lot of money here, and it will be safer in the bank."

"Why?" Yasmine asked again.

"Alhamdulillaah! You are full of questions! But these are good questions. Many adults don't even know enough to ask them," Lina smiled. *"The reason is because in our house, if there is a fire, your money will burn up. Or if, Allaah forbid, someone should break*

into our house, they could take your money. But a bank will keep it safe."

"What if there is a fire at the bank?" Yasmine wanted to know.

"Well, if there is a fire, the government guarantees your money. The bank keeps a computer record of how much money they have and who it belongs to. They also send you a bank statement that says how much money you have in the bank. If anything should happen to the bank, say it should go out of business, the government will pay you back all the money that was in the bank. Well, all up to $250,000. But I don't think you have to worry about having that much in the bank." Lina smiled again.

"So I should probably put my savings and Hajj fund in a bank too, right?"

"Right," Lina said. "The bank is open on Saturday morning. Your father can take you there and then you can stop by the computer store afterwards.

Early Saturday, Yasmine gathered up her fun jar, savings jar and Hajj jar. Her father had instructed her to count out the money in each one. Although the bank would count it out too, he said that it was good for her to have a record of the money she was taking. On a sheet of paper she listed each jar and the total in it. For her fun jar, she left $20 so she would have cash at home to spend.

Once counted, she placed the money back in the jars. The coins were dumped to the bottom while the bills were folded by denomination. Then Yasmine placed the jars in a small sack and went to the bank with Qadeer.

The process for opening an account was much longer than Yasmine anticipated. There was so much paperwork to fill out; and it had to done three times; since she wanted to open three accounts. Her savings and Hajj money went into savings accounts while it was decided that a checking account would be best for her fun money. Of course Yasmine was too young to open her own account so Qadeer had to co-sign for everything.

After the bank, the two drove to the local shopping district. The mall loomed ahead, but one of the smaller outbuildings was Qadeer's destination. Built like a giant box, the store was brightly lit with huge ceilings and bright signs on the door.

Inside, a sales associate greeted Yasmine immediately. Yasmine said 'Hi' and dropped her eyes from his gaze. Qadeer stepped up in response and explained the type of software that was needed. The employee turned and walked to an aisle in the center of the store. He showed Qadeer the programs available and then left them to consider their purchase.

"Well, your teacher was half right," Qadeer said. "You can get the basic version for $50, but the deluxe version is almost $100." He looked over the back of each box. "But I think you will be okay with the $50 version."

Trusting her father's judgment, Yasmine agreed. They walked to the front of the store to complete the purchase. Yasmine tucked the remaining money back into an envelope to be deposited the next time she visited the bank.

At home, she could hardly wait to try out the software. It seemed like an agonizing wait while Qadeer installed the software and set up the microphone. Finally, the system was ready to go. Yasmine spoke a few test phrases and was amazed to see them pop up on the screen.

Lina and Qadeer smiled at their daughter's joy and then left her in peace. Yasmine spent her remaining free time that day speaking into the microphone and watching her book come alive.

Chapter 6

Publishing The Book

"Mom, do we have any more printer paper?" Yasmine poked her head out of the den.

"Yes, there should be some in the bottom drawer of my desk," Qadeer said in reply.

"I already used that."

"All of it?"

"All of it...I'm sorry; I should have asked first," Yasmine looked down, ashamed that she didn't think to ask permission.

Qadeer stood up from his desk and walked towards the den. Lina was coming down the stairs. *"What are you printing to use so much paper?"* she asked.

"My book," Yasmine replied simply.

Lina hurried down the remaining steps, *"You're done?"*

Yasmine nodded as Lina walked past her to the den. It was now almost March, practically a year from when Yasmine first had the idea for her book. Lina had been living with her daughter's dream for so long that she had begun to think that there would never be an end in sight. But now, it appeared that all Yasmine's hard work was coming to an end.

In the den, Qadeer was pulling a huge stack of paper out of the printer. On the desk were three more stacks. *"Certainly, your book is not this long?"* Lina asked amazed. But in the back of her mind, she thought it certainly wasn't out of the realm of possibility. Yasmine had lived and breathed this book for almost a full year.

"No," Yasmine shook her head. *"It's 33 pages, but I want to print out 10 copies."*

Lina stifled a laugh, *"Oh, dear, that is a lot of paper. I don't think our little printer can handle all that."*

Qadeer didn't see the humor in the situation. He examined the printer carefully. It gave off a faint smell of burning plastic. Flipping through the most recent pages, he could also see that the ink cartridge was almost out. In spite of his frustration that his daughter had used all his paper and his ink, he was impressed that the cartridge had lasted that long.

Yasmine shrank against the far wall, waiting to be scolded. Qadeer muttered under his breath for Allaah (SWT) to give him strength. Then he turned to Yasmine. Instead of the scolding she expected, he smiled and said, *"Let's go to the copy shop."*

Later that day, Yasmine neatly arranged the 10 copies of her book on the kitchen table. The title *'Homeless No More'* was centered on the front page with Yasmine's name underneath. She beamed at her parents as they stood next to her.

"So, what's next?" Qadeer asked.

Yasmine shrugged, "I don't know…" She looked expectantly at her mom.

Lina thought for a moment, "I don't know either." She laughed lightly, "You're the first author in the family! Insha'Allaah, we'll figure out what to do."

Qadeer and Lina were sitting at the table following dinner that night. With her book done, Yasmine had taken the opportunity to use her newfound free time to start reading a new novel. She had been so involved in her homeless research that she hadn't done any reading for pleasure in months. Now that she started reading this book, she remembered how much she loved being transported to a whole new world through a good story.

While Yasmine sat in the living room, her parents talked quietly together. "Do you have any idea how a book is published?" Lina asked Qadeer.

"No," Qadeer answered, "other than that it is a hard process." He glanced into the living room. "I hope our Yasmine won't be too disappointed if she can't get it printed."

Lina sighed. She knew what Qadeer meant. Yasmine had poured her heart and soul into this book. She had flipped through one of the copies and thought her daughter's work was very good and that she showed wisdom beyond her years. However, Lina was also a realist and knew that many books were written and few were published. She hated to think of the heartache that would follow if the book wasn't printed.

"Let me talk to some people at work and see what they think," Qadeer suggested. Lina nodded in agreement, hoping that Allaah (SWT) would send some guidance their way.

The next night at dinner Qadeer shared his good news with the family, "I found a way to help publish Yasmine's book."

Yasmine, who had been picking at her food looked up in excitement, "What do I have to do?" she asked.

"I don't know," Qadeer replied. He held up his hand to stop her protest. "I don't know, but I think I have found someone who does." He paused for a moment to return to his dinner.

"Well, do tell us, Qadeer!" Lina said in exasperation.

Qadeer looked up at his wife. Then he turned to his daughter who was staring at him wide-eyed. He laughed softly. *"Okay, okay. I was speaking with Mr. Switalski who owns the butcher shop downtown. He sees so many different people through his store so I mentioned Yasmine's problem to him…"*

"And he told you what to do?" Yasmine interrupted.

"Do not interrupt your father," Lina reprimanded.

Qadeer continued, *"He said that he knew the woman who ran the local Chamber of Commerce. Apparently, there is a local author in the area, but Mr. Switalski didn't know his name; but the woman at the Chamber of Commerce does. So I called her and explained that my daughter was 8 and had written a book. It was finished, but she didn't know how to get it published."*

Stopping for a drink of water, Qadeer then continued, *"The woman at the Chamber of Commerce was very nice. She said that they were always happy to help young entrepreneurs…"*

Lina saw Yasmine's confused look. *"An entrepreneur is someone who runs their own business,"* she interjected.

Yasmine nodded and Qadeer waited. *"May I finish now?"* he asked.

"Yes, dear," Lina said. *"I am sorry for the interruption."*

"So the woman called the author, and he called me at the office. His name is Mr. Barnes. He writes historical biographies which is a bit different to what Yasmine has written. But he said he would be happy to look over her manuscript and give her some pointers on how to get published. I've made arrangements to take Yasmine to meet him on Saturday."

Lina sat back taking this all in. Yasmine smiled broadly at her father. Qadeer smiled back. *"So what do you think? You are all so quiet?"* he asked.

"I think it's wonderful. Thank you, Dad!" Yasmine jumped up to hug him.

Lina smiled from across the table. *"Allaahu Akbar,"* she said.

That Saturday, Qadeer and Yasmine pulled up to a cozy looking Cape Cod house at the end of a cul-de-sac. The house's front porch was adorned with a *Welcome* flag and crocuses grew by the steps. Yasmine thought it looked more like the type of home you would expect a grandmother to live in and not an author. Getting out of the car, Qadeer led the way up to the door and Yasmine followed.

A middle-aged woman with a bright apron answered the door with a smile. *"Hello,"* she said to Qadeer. Turning to Yasmine, she stated, *"And you must be Yasmine."*

Yasmine felt her courage leave her. She never liked meeting strangers and now she wished she could return to the car. Instead, she summoned all her strength and managed a small smile and a nod.

"Well, come on in," the woman said as she opened the door wide.

"Thank you," Qadeer said as he walked in. Yasmine followed close behind. Inside the house a stairway led to the second floor. To the right was a living room with a floral patterned couch and chair. Plush blue carpeting covered the floor except for a section immediately in front of a fireplace. Yasmine could see a candle burning on the mantle, and the room was lightly scented with lavender.

Directly ahead was the kitchen. *"Please come in and have a seat. May I offer you some water or lemonade?"* The woman looked kindly from Qadeer to Yasmine.

"Water, please," Qadeer requested.

When both adults turned to Yasmine, she quietly said, *"Lemonade, please."*

"Okay, coming right up," the woman turned to the refrigerator. *"Please, please, take a seat. Make yourself at home."* She turned back to Qadeer and Yasmine and gestured to the table. They sat on the wooden chairs with padded seats while waiting for their drinks.

The woman busily bustled through the kitchen, pulling out glasses and a serving tray. *"Larry tells me that you are only 8, Yasmine but you have written a book?"*

Yasmine wasn't sure who Larry was but she nodded yes.

"And what is it about?"

The woman set the lemonade in front of Yasmine and smiled kindly. Yasmine felt herself relax and took a sip of the drink. *"It's about homelessness."*

"Oooh, that's a big subject for a little girl!"

"I read for months before writing so I learned all about it. My book talks about why people are homeless and how others can help. I even wrote out ideas for kids who want to help." Yasmine explained her book to the attentive Mrs. Barnes.

"Very interesting, dear. Sounds like you've put a lot of work into it." She suddenly stood up from the table. *"Well, I suppose you want to meet the famous author."* She stood up giggling slightly. Opening a door with stairs leading downwards, she yelled, *"Larry, you have visitors."*

A moment later, a balding man emerged from the doorway. His voice boomed, *"Hello, hello!"* He walked to the table and bent over where Yasmine was sitting. *"You must be Yasmine!"* Mr. Barnes was a big man with a big voice. Yasmine shrank back in her chair.

Qadeer saw his daughter's discomfort and quickly stood. *"Hello, Mr. Barnes, I am Yasmine's father."* He held out his hand, and Mr. Barnes shook it heartily. With his other had, he clapped Qadeer on the shoulder. Mr. Barnes was a boisterous individual. Yasmine felt intimidated, but Qadeer smiled openly.

"Grab your drinks and let's go down to my office," Mr. Barnes said rubbing his hands together.

Yasmine looked nervously from Mr. Barnes to Mrs. Barnes to her dad. Qadeer picked up his glass. He bent over Yasmine and whispered in her ear, *"Don't be shy. I am right with you."*

After the airy openness of the kitchen, the basement was dark and cool. It had a slightly musty smell that reminded Yasmine of the books in her dad's den. Indeed, once they reached the bottom of the stairs Yasmine could see that Mr. Barnes also had quite the collection of books himself.

The stairs opened into a large room that was dimly lit. A desk was pushed against one wall, and bookshelves lined the walls. In the center there was a ragged old chair and an ottoman next to a small table. A slightly better looking couch sat opposite to the chair. On the tops of the bookshelves were model airplanes and ships. A coffee table was positioned between the couch and chair. It displayed a large replica battleship.

"Have a seat," Mr. Barnes motioned to the couch, *"Lily gets the upstairs when it comes to decorating, but the downstairs is my domain."* He took a seat in the ragged chair and swung his feet onto the ottoman. *"Now, tell me about your book, Yasmine."*

Yasmine looked at her hands for a moment while gathering her thoughts. She had decided that Mr. Barnes was nice, but he was loud. She reached into the backpack she had brought and pulled out a copy of her book; she handed it to Mr. Barnes.

"*Homeless No More,*" Mr. Barnes read to himself.

"*It's because that's what I want the book to do. I want it to make no more homeless people,*" Yasmine said suddenly.

"*Well, that is a fine goal, Yasmine,*" Mr. Barnes said. He flipped through the chapters. "*Now I hate to be the bearer of bad news, but if you plan to submit this as an unsolicited manuscript you'll have to change your spacing.*"

Yasmine didn't understand.

"*Editors like to see books with double-spacing so they can write notes and mark up what you've written,*" Mr. Barnes explained. With a wink, he added, "*Editors always thinking they can write too.*"

Yasmine understood about the spacing, but not about the manuscript. "*What does unsolicited mean?*"

Mr. Barnes set down the book, "*Well, there are unsolicited and solicited manuscripts. An unsolicited manuscript is one you send that the editor didn't ask for. You just put it in the mail, and hope for the best.*"

"*And a solicited one?*"

"*That's one that the editor has asked to see.*"

"*How would the editor know to ask for my book?*"

"*Well, usually, the writer sends what is called a query letter. Query basically means question, as in you are asking a question. And the question you are asking is, 'Will you read my manuscript?'*"

Yasmine nodded. She wished that she had brought some blank paper to write down notes. "*So it's probably better to have the editor ask for it?*"

Mr. Barnes thought for a moment, "*It really depends. You can send unsolicited manuscripts and they might end up in a slush pile never to be seen again. So it is good if the editor is waiting for it. But then, some publishers only want the whole thing. They don't want to be bothered with query letters.*"

"*How do you know who wants what?*" Yasmine asked.

"*Good question.*" Mr. Barnes stood up and walked to his desk. He pulled one of the drawers. "*There is this handy book that is published each year for writers. It lists all the book publishers and how they accept manuscripts. For some of them you need an agent, some have already decided what they are publishing this year and some only work with authors they've published in the past. You don't want to waste your time with any of those.*"

He handed the book to Yasmine to look through. *"Where can you buy this book?"* Qadeer wanted to know.

"Oh, you can get it at almost any bookstore or there is usually a copy in the library," Mr. Barnes shared.

Yasmine looked through Mr. Barne's dog-eared copy of the book. He had underlined some places, starred others and crossed out some. She could see where each entry listed the type of books that the publisher wanted. Some only printed fiction and some only children's books.

After a few more minutes, Qadeer stood and shook hands with Mr. Barnes. *"Thank you for your time. You have been most helpful."*

Mr. Barnes smiled at Yasmine, *"Let me know if you have any other questions. I'd love to be the first person to buy your book."*

Yasmine smiled in reply and climbed the stairs to the kitchen where Mrs. Barnes was sitting at the table looking through a magazine. She stood up and took the empty glasses from Qadeer and Yasmine. *"Did you have a nice visit?"*

Yasmine nodded as Qadeer said, *"Your husband was very helpful."*

"Good," Mrs. Barnes walked them to the door and wished them a good day. Yasmine skipped down the steps to the car.

Once she was buckled in, she turned to her dad, *"Can we go to the library now?"*

Qadeer glanced at the clock, *"No, it is too close to our time for prayer, and your mother will have dinner after that. You'll have to go another day."*

Disappointed, Yasmine turned to look out the window. Deep in thought, she was already writing the draft of her query letter in her mind.

The next day was Sunday, and the library was closed. Yasmine was anxious to start mailing her manuscript, and the day seemed to drag on forever. She tried reading but was too distracted. She milled around the house aimlessly. Eventually Lina sent her outside to play simply because her constant fidgeting was becoming an annoyance.

Originally, Lina had planned to take Yasmine to the library the following Saturday, but after that long Sunday, she relented and agreed that Yasmine could go after dinner on Monday. The library was open late that day. Lina gave a strict warning that if her

Qur'aan, Arabic and Islamic studies were not finished, the library would have to wait. Yasmine could barely contain her excitement, but she managed to focus on her studies after school. Then she squirmed in her seat until dinner was done. Rushing with the dishes afterwards, she tidied up the kitchen and then bounded upstairs to get a notebook.

Lina picked up the car keys and waited by the door. Yasmine ran by in a flash and was buckled before her mother had closed the door behind her. All the way there she beamed from ear to ear, imagining what it would be like to receive that letter stating her book was accepted.

At the library Yasmine was disappointed to see that her favorite librarian was not there. She approached a woman behind the desk and asked where she could find the reference book Mr. Barnes had showed her. The librarian searched on her computer and then walked to a shelf. Pulling it out, she informed Yasmine that it was a reference book and could not be checked out. Mr. Barnes had warned Yasmine about this so she came prepared with paper and a pencil.

Lina settled into one of the cozy chairs by the window. She had a stack of magazines that she flipped through one by one. Meanwhile, Yasmine sat in the far corner poring over the reference book.

Fortunately, the book was separated into sections that made it easy to find the publishers who might be interested in a book on homelessness. After skimming through the book once, Yasmine began writing. She continued until the librarian dimmed the lights to indicate closing time was near.

Yasmine stretched and put her pencil down. Lina also stood and stretched. She put away the magazines and checked on Yasmine's progress. *"Did you get what you needed?"*

"I think so," Yasmine said holding up the two papers. They were covered front and back with writing. *"This sheet,"* she shook the one in her right hand, *"has all the places that I think will definitely want the book. And this sheet,"* she shook the other hand, *"is my back-up list. But together, they should be more than enough."*

Yasmine smiled, and Lina smiled in return, *"I am sure they will be. Now it is time to get home. It is getting late."*

For the next week, Yasmine worked on her cover letters and query letters. Mr. Barnes had told her how important it was to write something that would catch the editor's attention. She wrote, read them to her parents and wrote some more.

Finally, she felt that they were done. Lina helped Yasmine carefully package the manuscript. She was sending out four unsolicited manuscripts and six query letters.

With much fanfare, Lina and Yasmine drove to the post office to mail the packages and letters. They sent them off and then stopped by the local candy store for a treat to celebrate.

Then Yasmine went home to wait.

Chapter 7

It's Not As Easy As It Looks

It became a daily ritual for Yasmine to wait for the mail. She had never been concerned with receiving anything before, but now she knew the postman's route like the back of her hand. If he didn't arrive by 11:30 AM, she began to compulsively check the window every five minutes.

Sundays and State holidays when the mail didn't run seemed the worst for Yasmine. The mail had become the highlight of her day, and when it would not arrive the hours seemed to drag on.

School ended and summer began; still no response to her mailings. Yasmine had contacted 10 publishers to start off, with the intention that she would go down the list to the next one as she received each response. She had always been sure that she wouldn't need to mail out any more. One of those initial publishers was bound to buy the book. In fact, Yasmine had spent quite some time thinking about what she would do in case more than one of them wanted to publish her work.

Now that months had passed without a response, she began to wonder if she shouldn't just start moving down the list and mailing to others. Or perhaps her manuscripts and letters had been lost in the mail, and she should resend them to the same publishers. Lina and Qadeer assured her that Mr. Barnes said it was not unusual to have to wait months to hear back from an editor.

Yasmine started third grade, and her days took on a regular schedule. She would wake up for the morning prayer (*Fajr*) and breakfast. After school, she would check the mail and say her afternoon prayers. This was followed by her practice of the Qur'aan, her Arabic and Islamic studies; then dinner, some reading and the night prayer. Throughout it all, in the back of her mind was the question of when or if she would receive a response about her book.

It was a sunny day in late September when the first response was finally received. Yasmine walked in from the cool air and greeted her mother. *"You received some mail today,"* Lina said.

"Mail?" Yasmine asked. *"Where?"*

"Two letters, they are sitting on the table."

Yasmine dropped her backpack with a thud and ran to the table. On it were two business size envelopes. Each addressed to her. She tore open the first one and read:

Dear Yasmine,

Thank you for sharing your manuscript. It is not every day that we receive work written by an 8 year old.

Unfortunately, while it is a worthy cause, we are not looking to publish any nonfiction books on the homeless issue this year.

I hope that you will continue your writing. Remember, the pen is mightier than the sword!

Best Regards,

Ernest Twier
Brooking Place Books

    Yasmine studied the letter for a moment and set it aside. She opened the next one and found a much less personal note inside.

Thank you for your correspondence.

We appreciate your time, but regret to inform you that we have elected not to request your full manuscript at this time.

Should this change, we will be back in touch with you.

Sincerely,

Landing Publishing

    Yasmine set this letter next to the first one. Lina picked them up and read each one over. She put her hand on Yasmine's shoulder, and her daughter looked up at her. *"I'm sorry, honey."*
    Clearly let down, Yasmine shrugged and said, *"It's okay, I still have lots of other places on my list to send the book."*

Lina smiled, *"That's right."*

After dinner, Yasmine went to Qadeer's study and wrote up letters for the next two publishers on her list. Both were query letters, and she carefully signed and folded each one. Placing stamps on the corner of each envelope, she said a small prayer and placed them in the mailbox for the next day's pick-up.

When she came home from school on the following day, she found another response from a publisher. It was a small postcard that simply said,

We have received your submission to Willow Tree Books.

We are not currently accepting new manuscripts.

Thank you.

Yasmine sighed and filed the postcard with the letters in a folder. She crossed Willow Tree Books off her list and moved down to the next publisher on the list.

Months passed and the letters continued to arrive. Sometimes they were friendly and personable like Mr. Twier's letter and sometimes they were photocopied form letters. But they all said the same thing; thanks but no thanks.

Two of the publishers from the initial batch of 10 never responded, and Yasmine eventually crossed them off the list, giving up hope. After she had mailed everyone on her list, she made another trip to the library to write down more publishers. This was followed by three more trips to the library.

The folder with the rejection letters and postcards became thicker and thicker. First it had 10, then 20, then 100 letters. Yasmine could barely look at the milk crate with her carefully compiled research and remaining manuscripts.

It was spring now, and the tree buds were blossoming up and down the street. It should be a time of awakening and renewal, but Yasmine could only feel the dull ache of rejection. She trudged home from the bus each day and never bothered to check the mail anymore.

On this particular day it was raining sheets of rain. She walked into the house and removed her boots and coat. Lina emerged from the kitchen as she always did when she heard

Yasmine arrive, *"Assalamu-alaykum, my dear,"* she said with her signature smile.

Yasmine couldn't bring herself to smile, but said, *"Wa'alaykum assalaam,"* anyway. The gloomy day clouded her already poor spirits.

"Do you want your mail now?" Lina asked.

"No, it's all the same thing anyway," Yasmine mumbled under her breath as she headed up to her room.

Lina followed her, carrying the letter. She stood in the doorway of Yasmine's room and watched as the girl threw herself on her bed, burying her head in her pillow. Small sobs could be heard, and Lina's chest tightened. She hated to see her daughter in pain. She couldn't help but wonder if this was her fault. Had she pushed too hard? Had she not prepared Yasmine with realistic expectations?

She walked to the bed and sat down at Yasmine's side. She rubbed her back while praying for the right thing to say, but words escaped her. Yasmine rolled to her side and looked up with tear-streaked cheeks. *"It's no use! I am an awful writer! I spent months on that dumb book and no one likes it!"* Yasmine wailed.

Lina shook her head, *"No, no, never say that."* She bent over to hug Yasmine and then pulled back to wipe away her tears. *"You are a bright, compassionate and faithful child. Your book is wonderful, and I don't just say that as your mother. I read it myself and shared copies with my friends. They all thought it was great. And most importantly, I pray that Allaah (SWT) is pleased with your work. Ameen.*

"But you must remember, Yasmine that thousands of people write books each year and there are only so many that can be published. And publishers aren't always looking for the best books; they are looking for the books that will make them the most money. You can't take it personally."

Yasmine didn't look convinced, but she nodded.

"Insha'Allaah," Lina continued, *"we must simply pray. If it is Allaah's Will it will be published. If it is not, then we must accept His Will. Understood?"*

Yasmine nodded a little more confidently this time. She sat up on the bed and grabbed a tissue from the box on her end table. *"I don't think it is Allaah's (SWT) Will then. I am almost through with* all the publishers in the book, and I still haven't found one that likes it. Allaah (SWT) must not want it published."

Looking at the letter in her hand, Lina replied, *"That is a possibility. But it could also be that Allaah wants you to try a little harder. Maybe you just need to be creative."*

"Like how?"

"I don't know. But if it is meant to be, Allaah will show you a way." Lina leaned over again to kiss her daughter. She touched her wet *hijaab, "You must get changed. You are soaking wet!"* Then she left to let Yasmine consider her words in silence.

Yasmine did not send out any more manuscripts that week. Her mood seemed to brighten somewhat but instead of being cheery, she appeared deep in thought. At prayer times she appeared particularly intense.

Lina had told Qadeer about her conversation with Yasmine, and he advised her to leave their daughter be for a while. *"She must work this out with Allaah (SWT). It is not for us to interfere."*

After nearly two weeks with no discussion of the book, Yasmine asked her father at the dinner table, *"Do you think I could go see Mr. Barnes again?"*

Qadeer was surprised at the question, but recovered his composure. *"Mr. Barnes? I don't see why not. He said he was interested to hear about your progress."*

"Good," said Yasmine returning to her dinner.

Qadeer looked across the table to Lina, *"I'll call tomorrow and see if we can go out on Saturday."*

Yasmine continued to eat her dinner and did not say another thing about the book for the rest of the week.

On Saturday Qadeer and Yasmine once again drove up to the snug Cape Cod. Yasmine didn't have the same fear that she had felt during their first visit. She was on a mission, and she was sure that Mr. Barnes was the person to help her.

Back in the basement, Yasmine sat on the edge of the couch and looked earnestly at Mr. Barnes, *"No one wants to publish my book."*

"Oh," said Mr. Barnes, *"I am sorry to hear that, but it is something every author has encountered."* Qadeer had briefed Mr Barnes on Yasmine's progress prior to their visit so he was not caught off-guard.

"That's what my mom and dad told me," Yasmine said.

"Uh huh," Mr. Barnes clearly did not have any comforting words for Yasmine.

Undaunted, she continued, *"Is there any other way to publish my book? I think it's an important subject and my book will help people."*

"Hmmmm…," Mr. Barnes thought for a moment. *"Well, there is another way to publish a book, but I am not sure it will work for you."*

Yasmine waited impatiently for him to continue.

"You could self-publish the book," Mr. Barnes finally said.

"What is self-publishing?" The light returned to Yasmine's eyes. She was sure that this was the answer she was seeking.

Mr. Barnes looked from Yasmine to Qadeer, *"Well, self-publishing is where you print the book yourself."*

Qadeer snorted, *"Print it ourselves? On our printer?"*

"Oh heavens no!" Mr. Barnes laughed hysterically. *"No, no, no…you'd never sell a book you print on your home printer."*

Yasmine glanced between her father, who looked slightly offended, and Mr. Barnes who was trying desperately to control his laughter.

Taking a drink from the glass in front of him, Mr. Barnes finally calmed himself. *"I am so sorry,"* he apologized to Qadeer, *"to self-publish, you pay someone to print it for you. Some companies will even do cover art and some minor marketing for you."*

"Do these books sell?" Qadeer asked, *"or are they just a trophy for someone to put on their bookshelf so they can say they wrote a book?"*

Mr. Barnes stood up and walked to his bookshelf. *"Oh, no, they can sell. It all depends on how much effort you put into it."* He pulled out a book and returned to his chair.

"Now, some authors get pretty high and mighty about self-published books," Mr. Barnes continued. *"They seem to think that any 'real' author wouldn't pay to have their book printed. But that's all elitist hogwash. See here…"*

He handed Qadeer a book with a photo of a man in a military uniform on the front. *"That's my first book,"* Mr. Barnes explained. *"No one would buy it, even though it's darn good if I do say so myself. I sent it to everyone and their brother. Got a stack of rejection letters this high,"* Mr. Barnes held his hands about a foot apart.

Yasmine was very excited now. This sounded just like her stack of rejection letters.

"So I figured, forget them. I'll do it myself. It was a lot of work, and I had to do all the selling myself. I couldn't get the big chain bookstores to stock, but Mr. Jenkins downtown did, even though he has a used bookstore. He even let me come in and do a book signing event.

"I sent copies to the paper and some magazines and got some reviews there as well. Between that and the word of mouth, I sold about 1500 copies of that book. Not too shabby for a first timer, if I do say so myself," Mr. Barnes slapped his knee, obviously pleased with himself.

"And you know the best thing?" He lowered his voice and leaned in towards Yasmine. *"The best thing is that an editor read a review of my book and bought a copy. And then he sent me a letter asking for my next manuscript. He published that book and has been my editor ever since!"*

There, it was that! This was the answer Yasmine was looking for! She was sure of it. Oh, thank you, thank you, thank you Allaah (SWT), she thought in her head. Practically bouncing in her seat, Yasmine asked, *"Mr. Barnes, how do I find a self-publishing company? Is it in the book you showed me?"*

Mr. Barnes shook his head, *"No, they aren't listed there. But you can find them online. I'll send you home with a couple of links to places on the internet that specialize in self-publishing."*

Qadeer had been quiet through all this and now the author and the author-to-be looked over at him. His brow furrowed and he absentmindedly pulled at his eyebrow. Realizing the room was suddenly silent, he looked up. *"I just don't know,"* he said.

"Why not?" Yasmine demanded.

"Because it is probably quite expensive to print your own book; I doubt you have that much saved, and it's not something your mother and I have extra money for."

"Then I'll just do more cleaning," Yasmine insisted.

"It might take you years to raise the money from cleaning," Qadeer stated.

Yasmine could feel her frustration rising. Here, she had her answer and her father would not help. She crossed her arms and plopped back on the couch.

Sensing the tension between father and daughter, Mr. Barnes interjected, *"Well, there are lots of ways to go about it."*

Yasmine shifted her attention from Qadeer to Mr. Barnes. He continued, *"There are some places were you can buy a run of books. Say a couple hundred. You pay for them upfront and then keep the money as you sell them. Then there are other places that do what is called 'Print on Demand'. You pay them a fee to set up your book and then people order directly off the website. The money goes to the company that does the printing and you get a cut of the profits."*

He had both Qadeer and Yasmine's attention now. *"It's cheaper that way – no inventory, but it also makes it harder to market. It's not like you can have a stash of books in your trunk to sell to family and friends. Well, I guess you could buy them from a 'Print on Demand' place, but you'll probably pay more per book."*

Yasmine's mind was swimming with the possibilities. Mr. Barnes wrote down the web addresses for several companies and sent them on their way. Yasmine chattered the whole way home, excited to once again talk about her book. Qadeer kept his thoughts to himself. Although excited for Yasmine, he was worried that his daughter would once again be set up for disappointment.

Late that night, Qadeer and Lina sat side by side at the computer. Qadeer looked up each web address and reviewed the company's benefits and costs. While Yasmine was allowed to use the computer, Qadeer was always careful to prescreen any websites before she visited them. It had become an unfortunate reality that the internet, like the TV, had become largely unsuitable for modest people.

They talked in hushed voices about the information on each site. Both shared the same concern; that Yasmine would either be unable to afford the printing or she would pay for it and still not sell any books.

After crossing off one site that featured romance novels and their excerpts prominently on its homepage, Yasmine's parents gave her the green light to check the sites the next day. Lina sat with Yasmine as she scanned the pages and read all the frequently asked questions.

"Most of this doesn't tell you how much it costs," Yasmine complained.

"We noticed that last night," Lina agreed.

Many of the 'Print on Demand' sites did have basic costs listed, but by and large all companies required that you contact their representative for a quote. *"Why don't you pick the two you like the best, and we'll contact them for a quote."*

Yasmine agreed but took the next two days to decide. She finally presented her two options to her parents. *"These are both more traditional self-publishing companies,"* Qadeer observed. *"I think it will be more realistic to use a 'Print on Demand' site."*

But Yasmine would not be deterred, *"I want to have some books to sell myself."* Qadeer looked at her skeptically. She continued on, *"It's like Mr. Barnes said; when you publish your own book you have to market it yourself. I can't go to bookstores with no books."*

Qadeer looked at Lina. His wife offered a compromise, *"Well, let's see how much it costs and then Yasmine can decide from there."*

Since Yasmine was just 9 and did not have her own email address, her parents sent off messages to both companies. Then, as had been the case so often during this process, Yasmine waited for a response.

The first one came the next day. It asked for more information about the length of the book, whether cover art was needed and the type of binding Yasmine would like. The answer went back immediately; the book was 33 pages, art was needed and Yasmine would like a quote on both hardcover and soft cover books.

The response from the second company arrived several days later. It came in the form of a table that listed prices based upon the number of books printed and the binding type. Yasmine's jaw dropped when she saw the prices. She had expected that the several hundred dollars she had in the bank would cover most of the cost; but the fee from the company would be almost ten times as much.

The second quote arrived the following day and was even higher. Lina and Qadeer were concerned that Yasmine's gloom would return. There was simply no way that Yasmine could pay for the cost of printing.

"Can't you pay some of it, and I'll pay you back?" Yasmine asked.

Qadeer shook his head, *"Going into debt is no way to start a business. We will be happy to give you some money to help with the cost, but it will be a gift with no repayment expected."*

Before Yasmine could get too excited, he added, *"But we can only match what you have in the bank. There is no way we can afford the entire cost."*

Yasmine looked to Lina, *"Mom, can't you please?"* she pleaded.

"I'm sorry, Yasmine," Lina said gently. *"It's not that we don't want to, but we simply don't have the money."*

"Come here," Qadeer motioned Yasmine to the den. *"Now, we don't often talk about our family's money with you, but I think you are old enough to understand."*

He sat at the computer and moved the mouse to open a new program. Lines flashed across the screen and numbers filled the lines. *"What's that?"* Yasmine asked in amazement.

"This, my dear, is a spreadsheet," Qadeer said smiling. *"I use them all the time at work. I also use one for our family budget."*

"And what's our family budget?"

Lina joined the two at the computer and answered, *"Our family budget is what we use to make sure we pay all our bills each month and that we are spending our money wisely."*

Qadeer pointed to a number near the top of the screen. *"See this here…that's how much money I make each month. We have to use that money to pay for the house, our electricity, our food, our zakaah."*

"Wow!" Yasmine exclaimed, *"We're rich!"*

Qadeer laughed, *"Not quite. It doesn't go as far as you might think. This is what we pay each month for the house. Here's our money for the groceries. We have to pay for electricity, water and heat. Then, we set some aside for new clothes as needed; gasoline for our car, and so on…and down here, you see there is not much left at the end of the month."*

"Oh," Yasmine said.

"So you see, Yasmine," Lina put her hands on the girl's shoulders, *"it is not that we don't want to help you, but we simply don't have the extra money in our budget to pay for such a high publishing cost."*

"Okay, I understand," Yasmine sighed.

The family walked back out into the living room. *"If you want to self-publish your book,"* Lina said, *"you should think about doing a new business plan."*

"Why?"

"Because now you have a big expense; a business plan can help you figure out how to pay for that expense. You'll also need to figure out how much to charge for your book once it is published. The business plan will tell you your expenses so you can determine how much revenue you must make before reaching a profit."

As her mom talked, Yasmine walked to the desk that held her school work. She opened a top drawer and pulled out her original business plan; the one that Lina and her had created years ago when she was 6 and started doing housework. Now, she was 9, and she studied the sheet. She smiled as she remembered all the work that went into it.

"Do you want me to help you with it?" Lina asked.

"I think I've got it, Mom, but I'll let you know if I get stuck," Yasmine answered.

With a business plan done, Yasmine carefully reviewed all her current finances. She decided that her savings account would serve only for the book right now. She had never given up hope of getting her American Bobtail, but the dream of her book surpassed that of her cat.

Lina and Yasmine made a visit to the bank, and she transferred most of her checking account to savings. Lina also gifted Yasmine with a check that she deposited into the savings. With that money she had about a quarter of what she would need for the book printing.

Another school year was coming to a close, and Yasmine was anxious for summer to arrive. *"Why are you in such a rush?"* Mrs. Chrisman asked her one day. *"When it is summer I won't be able to see you. I will miss our morning chats."*

Yasmine and Sydney still stopped by to see Mrs. Chrisman each morning, and the teacher counted the girls as among her most cherished students.

"I need to do more cleaning," Yasmine explained.

Momentarily confused, Mrs. Chrisman gave Yasmine a strange look, *"You can't wait for school to get over so you can do more chores?"*

"For my cleaning business," Yasmine said.

"Oh!" It had been so long since Yasmine had mentioned her cleaning business that Mrs. Chrisman had forgotten. It seemed as though the last year had revolved around her book instead. *"I haven't heard much about that lately. I wasn't sure you were still doing it,"* her former teacher said, looking sheepish.

"Well, I wasn't doing much for a while because I was writing the book, but I need to earn some money now."

"What do you want to buy?"

"I need money to publish my book."

"Isn't it supposed to be the other way around? Aren't the publishers supposed to pay you?" Sydney said as she skipped up to the two.

Yasmine looked at Sydney and answered, *"Mr. Barnes says that it is really, really hard for new writers to get published so sometimes you have to self-publish at first."*

"I see," Sydney looked at Mrs. Chrisman. *"Have a good summer, Mrs. Chrisman."*

"I plan to," she smiled at both girls. *"I will see you girls next year. Good luck with your book, Yasmine!"* With that, she turned and walked down the hall to the office.

Sydney and Yasmine walked towards the bus silently. *"So you have to work all summer to raise money for your book?"* the younger girl asked.

Yasmine nodded, *"Looks like it. Mom and Dad don't think I'll be able to raise much, but I think if I start helping some of the neighbors I'll do okay."*

Reaching into her pocket Sydney pulled out a crinkled $5 bill, *"Here, take this,"* she offered.

Yasmine pushed her hand away, *"I couldn't take your money."*

But Sydney insisted, *"Really, I know it's not much, but I want to help. Will you take it, please?"*

"Okay," Yasmine relented. She smiled at her best friend, *"Thanks."* The two girls hugged and then separated to walk to their own buses. *"I'll miss you,"* Yasmine called out.

"I'll miss you too," Sydney yelled as she waved and boarded the final afternoon bus of the school year.

Chapter 8

When One Door Closes, 10 More Open!

Once summer began Yasmine's schedule took on a new routine. She moved her Qur'aan, Arabic and Islamic studies to the morning after prayer and breakfast. Despite Yasmine's request to take the summer off from studying, Lina insisted.

"You might not appreciate it now, but these are the most important subjects you can learn." Lina looked in her daughter's pleading eyes. *"You may be able to take a summer off from Math and Science, but you should never take time off from Allaah's (SWT) Word."*

So Yasmine continued her studies in the morning and spent her afternoons cleaning. She developed a regular circuit of jobs. On Mondays she helped Mrs. McKenzie. On Tuesday she was at the Smiths down the street. Wednesday and Thursday, she was at home with her mom, and Friday alternated between the Leiner family and the Price family.

The money added up but it came at a slow pace. Yasmine was beginning to realize that her parents were right; she would never earn the money through cleaning alone.

It was a beautiful June day when Qadeer came home smiling. He set down his briefcase and greeted his wife and daughter.

"You are in an awfully chipper mood," Lina laughed.

"That's right! Today was a fabulous day. The type of day where everything went as planned!" He smiled as he unpacked some papers. Then he looked at Yasmine, *"I have some news for you as well."*

"Me?" Yasmine said. She had been helping Lina with dinner preparations, but now she stopped and wiped her hands on a towel. *"What news do you have for me?"*

"Well, I received a call from Mr. Barnes today," Qadeer looked expectantly at Yasmine. *"He is a member of the Rotary Club. It's a group of businesspeople who meet for lunch and they have speakers and so on."*

"And what does that have to do with Yasmine?" Lina asked.

"They just started a new Junior Rotarian program. It is so students can join with the businesspeople and learn from them. Rub shoulders with the experts so to speak."

Yasmine spoke up, *"And I get to go?"*

"The program is really geared for high school students, but Mr. Barnes asked if you could be his guest. He thought you might

meet some people who could help with your book. Are you interested?" Qadeer concluded.

"Of course I am! Alhamdulillaah!" Yasmine jumped up and down.

"Good because I told him you would be. I will come with you, and we'll have lunch with the Rotary Club each Monday for as long you'd like."

"Won't that interfere with your work, Qadeer?" Lina questioned.

Qadeer shook his head. "They meet during lunch right down the street from my office, but it would be helpful if you could get Yasmine downtown for me."

It was agreed that Yasmine would become a Junior Rotarian. Her first meeting was the following week. She put on her nicest outfit and *hijaab*. Lina drove her to City Hall where the meeting would take place. "I'll drop you off and then be back to pick you up afterwards."

Yasmine saw her father waiting by the steps, "There's Dad!"

Lina pulled up to the curve, and Yasmine hopped out. She waved to her husband before pulling away to run her own errands.

"Are you ready?" Qadeer asked as he held open the door.

Yasmine's stomach felt like it was in her throat, but she nodded yes. Her excitement was mixed with nervous anticipation. She had no idea what to expect. Would she have to talk? Would everyone stare at her? She moved closer to her dad as they followed the sign pointing to the meeting place.

It was a large conference room scattered with round tables throughout the floor. Each table was elegantly set with linens, silverware, salads and rolls. A sea of people was spread out among the tables. They were gathered in clusters here and there, standing together and talking loudly.

Yasmine scanned the room and saw several faces she recognized from local stores. There were also many whom she did not recognize. Men in suits and women dressed in blazers and skirts. At a table near the center, she noticed Mr. Barnes talking to a woman. The woman apparently noticed Qadeer and Yasmine and nodded in their direction.

Mr. Barnes turned and walked briskly extending his hand. "Good to see you, Qadeer! Good to see you!" As he spoke, he pumped Qadeer's hand in an exaggerated motion and clapped him on the shoulder several times. Everything about Mr. Barnes seemed big and loud. Yasmine had been so intimidated by him when they first met, but now she found that his quirky behavior made him endearing.

Qadeer reclaimed his hand and thanked Mr. Barnes for inviting them.

"You should be a member here yourself, Qadeer. You own your own accounting business. You belong here," Mr. Barnes rubbed his hands together as he was talking.

"Hi, Mr. Barnes," Yasmine spoke up.

"Oh, Yasmine! I am sorry; I didn't mean to ignore you," Mr. Barnes looked down at her. *"I hope you'll have a good time and learn something new here. The talk today is about business taxes which might bore you, but at least the food is good. It's catered by a local restaurant; it's fantastic, and we always have a great dessert."*

Mr. Barnes smiled and laughed. Qadeer smiled at Yasmine, *"So it sounds like today we will feast!"* Yasmine nodded and looked back at the table.

"Yup, today, we are having pork chops I think," Mr. Barnes said.

Yasmine wrinkled her nose. Pork was unclean meat; she couldn't eat pork! Qadeer leaned in to whisper something to Mr. Barnes. His smile disappeared for a moment. Then it returned, *"There's always a vegetarian dish – will that work?"*

Qadeer nodded, and Mr. Barnes spotted a woman in a black apron filling water glasses. *"Excuse me,"* he said to Qadeer and Yasmine. "Mandy...," he called out as he walked to the woman.

When Mr. Barnes had left, Yasmine tugged on her dad's arm. *"Dad, we can't eat pork chops. We should leave..."*

Putting his finger to his lips, Qadeer motioned for Yasmine to be quiet. He whispered, *"Don't worry; Mr. Barnes is taking care of it."*

Mr. Barnes returned and announced, *"Eggplant Parmesan! How about that?"*

Yasmine didn't know what Eggplant Parmesan was, but Qadeer said, *"That sounds fine."*

Someone tapped a glass and the room quieted. A man near a podium asked everyone to take their seats. Mr. Barnes led Qadeer and Yasmine to a table in the middle of the room. Yasmine was excited to see that Mr. Jenkins, the bookstore owner, was at their table.

The man at the podium made several announcements and mentioned that today marked the first lunch with the Junior Rotarians. Yasmine felt her face flush hot red as everyone at the table turned to stare at her. After that it was time to eat.

Mr. Barnes made the introductions at the table. Yasmine was surprised that her father seemed to know everyone there. At dinner that night, he told her that as an accountant he worked for many of the small business owners' downtown. In addition to Mr. Jenkins, there were owners of a landscape business, an auto repair shop and a bath and beauty store. But the person who most caught Yasmine's attention was the final guest at the table.

"This is Mrs. Jane Wildey," Mr. Barnes introduced the woman he had been talking to when Qadeer and Yasmine arrived. *"She runs the Guiding Light Shelter."*

Yasmine gave a small gasp, and Mrs. Wildey smiled warmly, *"It is a pleasure to meet you."* Yasmine liked her already.

"What a coincidence!" Qadeer pretended to be surprised, although it was obvious that Mr. Barnes had arranged for both Mr. Jenkins and Mrs. Wildey to be at Yasmine's table.

"It is not every day that I get to sit down to such a nice lunch with one of our regular contributors," she looked at Yasmine.

In slight disbelief, Yasmine raised her neck, *"You mean me?"*

"That's right," Mrs. Wildey said. *"You've been sending up money monthly for the last several years if I recall correctly."*

"It's my sadaqah; money from my cleaning business to help those who are not as fortunate," Yasmine explained.

Mr. Jenkins nodded in understanding.

Mrs. Wildey continued, *"Well, Yasmine, trust me that we have worked hard to put your donations to good use. It is because of generous people like you that many in our city have a warm bed and meal to wake up to in the morning."*

A server began to clear off the salad plates while a second approached with dinner dishes. It was Mandy, the woman Mr. Barnes had spoken to earlier. She placed plates in front of Yasmine and Qadeer. It had a pasta dish she had never eaten before. Yasmine was embarrassed to see that they were the only two at the table with food in front of them.

She wasn't sure if she should start eating; she felt awkward. But her father didn't start eating so she followed his lead. Another server placed plates of pork chops in front of the other guests. Yasmine tried hard not to make a face. She couldn't imagine someone eating that. Mandy returned with another pasta plate and put it in front of Mrs. Wildey.

"Oh," Yasmine said automatically, *"you don't eat pork either?"*

Qadeer put his hand on Yasmine's arm, but Mrs. Wildey just laughed. *"Actually, I don't eat any kind of meat. Just not for me."*

Regardless of the reason why, Yasmine felt much better that someone else at the table was also eating pasta. It also made her that much more enthralled with Mrs. Wildey.

Throughout the meal, the guests at the table talked about Yasmine's book, and her plans to self-publish. When the delicious chocolate cake was served for dessert, a speaker gave a presentation about business taxes. As Mr. Barnes had predicted, it was boring. At the end of the presentation, everyone stood, shook hands and continued on with their day.

Mrs. Wildey walked out with Yasmine and Qadeer, *"I have an idea that might help you raise money to publish your book."*

Yasmine was all ears.

"The shelter sends out a monthly newsletter. How about we see if we can put an article in the newsletter about your book and ask for donations," Mrs. Wildey suggested.

"You would do that for me?" Yasmine asked excitedly.

"I don't know, Yasmine...," Qadeer looked doubtful. *"I don't know if I like the idea of asking strangers for money."*

Mrs. Wildey waved her hand, *"It would be no bother at all. It is the least we can do for one of our longtime supporters."* She smiled at Yasmine who looked expectantly at her father.

Qadeer thought for a moment and then said, *"All right, but I would be more comfortable if we could see the article before it was published."*

"Oh, of course!" Mrs. Wildey assured him. She took the family phone number and then said good-bye as she walked down the street. Lina was waiting in the car by the curb. Yasmine gave Qadeer a quick kiss before jumping into the car.

As they traveled home, Yasmine excitedly shared all about the lunch event with her mother.

Mrs. Wildey called the next night and set up a time to meet with Yasmine. Lina drove her downtown and the three of them walked around the shelter. It was largely empty, and Mrs. Wildey explained that there was a cleaning period during the day when everyone was asked to leave.

They then returned to Mrs. Wildey's office. It was a small room with a basic desk and chair. A corkboard on the wall held several photos and a calendar. Lina had often heard that in some charities, the directors lived like kings and queens; but that did not seem to be the case at the Guiding Light Shelter.

A young woman named Marie joined them in the office. *"Marie is our intern and writes the newsletter articles,"* Mrs. Wildey shared. Marie asked Yasmine a number of questions and took ample notes. Then she had Yasmine stand by a wall to have her photograph taken.

"You will let us see what you have written before it is printed, right?" Lina confirmed.

"Right," said Mrs. Wildey. She took down Lina's email address and promised that the article would arrive the following week.

It did, and Lina printed a copy of the article to share with Yasmine and Qadeer.

LOCAL GIRL WRITES BOOK ON HOMELESSNESS

While other girls her age may be riding bikes and playing with toys, 9 year old Yasmine is concerned with the bigger issues of the world. Wanting to make a difference in the world, she decided that something needed to be done about the homeless of the world.

As Yasmine explains, "I couldn't imagine not having my own bed to sleep in each night." Her desire to help others led her through a year-long process of reading and writing her own book, *Homeless No More*.

At Guiding Light Shelter, we were fortunate enough to preview a copy of the book. It is a touching story of why

homelessness exists and, more importantly, what we can do about it.

Unfortunately, Yasmine has learned the hard way that breaking into the world of publishing can be difficult for a young writer. She is currently pursuing self-publishing options and is raising funds to make her dream a reality.

If you would like to help make Yasmine's dream come true, we at Guiding Light Shelter encourage you to make a donation to this worthy cause.

Donations may be sent to *Homeless No More*, c/o Guiding Light Shelter...

Lina looked up from the article, *"So, what do you think?"*
"I like it," said Yasmine.
"I do too," Lina agreed. *"Qadeer?"*
Mother and daughter looked at Qadeer. He nodded slowly and said, *"Yes, I think that sounds just fine."*
"Hooray!" Yasmine shouted.
A copy of the newsletter came a week later. Yasmine carried it around the house with her all day. There she was, on the front cover. She read the words over and over until she had memorized every word.

"Their reward is with Allaah: Gardens of Eternity beneath which rivers flow; They will dwell therein for ever; Allaah well pleased with them, and they with Him: all this for such as fear their Lord and Cherisher."

(The Qur'aan: Chapter 98, Verse 8)

The current verse Yasmine was studying ran through her mind over and over again. *Insha'Allaah* was the words always on her lips. During each of the day's *salaahs* she thanked Allaah (SWT) and asked for His Blessings. All the while, a separate thought was forming in her head.

The idea of asking others to help pay for her book had not crossed her mind until Mrs. Wildey suggested it. Now, she wondered if there would be others would be willing to donate. She often saw in the paper about wealthy people who donated to various causes. By *Fajr salaah*, Yasmine had decided that she would draft a letter to famous people she knew who had money, in the hopes that they too would donate to her cause. *Allaahu Akbar*, she whispered to herself.

After finishing her Islamic studies the next day, Yasmine had some free time before lunch. She sat down with her notebook and wrote out all the famous people she knew who seemed like the people who would donate money. Her list wasn't long but it included only the biggest names:

Bill Gates
Warren Buffet
Oprah Winfrey
Angelina Jolie/Brad Pitt
Yusuf Islam (Cat Stevens)
Omar Sharif
Muhammad Ali

Taking it to Lina, she explained her plans. Lina looked doubtful. *"I don't want to discourage you but I don't know if any of these people even open their own mail, let alone respond to requests for money."*

"But it wouldn't hurt, would it, Mom?"

"I suppose not...," Lina responded, slowly.

"Great!" Yasmine ran upstairs before Lina could say another word.

With Yasmine upstairs, Lina sat on the couch looking at the list in her hand. She couldn't imagine how to even find the addresses of these people, and she certainly didn't want Yasmine trolling around the internet for them.

Walking to the den, Lina fired up the computer and got online. To her amazement, it took less than one minute of searching to find a website that listed fan mailing addresses for everyone on Yasmine's list. *Alhamdulillaah*, Lina muttered as she wrote down the addresses for each celebrity and philanthropist.

Returning to the kitchen, she placed the list on the table and returned to her lunch preparation. She called up to Yasmine and sat the lunch plates on the table.

Yasmine bounded into the room and picked up the sheet on the table. Her eyes lit up when she realized what her mom had done. *"Oh, thank you!"* she squealed with delight as she hugged Lina.

The next day, Yasmine placed 7 carefully addressed letters in the mailbox. But by that afternoon, it was discovered that the letters probably weren't needed.

Mrs. Wildey called excitedly about midday and asked if she could come over. When she arrived, Lina greeted her at the door and motioned her to the kitchen. Mrs. Wildey hurried to the table carrying a stack of envelopes.

Yasmine's eyes went wide when she saw the envelopes. She was sure that this was Allaah's (SWT) answer to her prayers. Mrs. Wildey collected herself and caught her breath as Yasmine and Lina gathered around her.

"Guess what these are?" Mrs. Wildey asked Yasmine.

"Donations for my book," Yasmine said hopefully.

"Right!" Mrs. Wildey exclaimed. *"And that's exciting enough, I know."* She spread the envelopes across the table. *"Most of these came with $10-$25 donations inside. But this one...,"* Mrs. Wildey reached into her purse *"this one is different."*

She set it on the table. It had a typed address and the return address had a gold foil stamp next to it. Lina gasped when she saw it. *"What is it, Mom?"* Yasmine wanted to know.

"This is what you've been waiting for, Yasmine," Mrs. Wildey said dramatically putting her finger on the envelope. She picked it up and waved it in the air, her smile becoming progressively bigger. *"Did you know that the Governor's wife sometimes donates to the Guiding Light Shelter?"*

"No," Yasmine answered. She was excited by the envelope but also confused by what Mrs. Wildey was trying to tell her.

"Well, she has occasionally. She has a great aunt who lives in the area. But anyways, she is on our mailing list, and this arrived today." Mrs. Wildey gave the letter one final shake.

"And...," Lina said impatiently.

"And she thinks Yasmine's book is a great idea," Mrs. Wildey said triumphantly.

Yasmine smiled. It was certainly nice that the Governor's wife thought her book was worthwhile.

"Not only that," the shelter director continued, *"she has offered to pay whatever you need to publish your book."*

The room erupted with cheering and laughter. Yasmine jumped up and down and then hugged Mrs. Wildey. Lina wiped away a tear from her eye as she read over the letter she took from Mrs. Wildey's hand. *"Alhamdulillaah, alhamdulillaah, Allaahu Akbar! Allaahu Akbar!"* she repeated over and over again.

Chapter 9

The Boxes

The next month was a whirlwind of activity. Mrs. Wildey coordinated everything with the Governor's office. Lina helped Yasmine pick out the right publishing package and sent away the contract. When the proof arrived, Yasmine invited Mr. Barnes and Mrs. Wildey to review it. Together, the group pored over the sample to make sure it was absolutely perfect.

On a late August day when the air hang heavy and the high pitched shrill of cicadas seemed to fill the sky, a brown truck pulled up in front of Yasmine's house. A delivery man hopped out of the truck and walked to the house. He rang the bell. *"Delivery from On Call Publishing,"* he said when Lina answered.

"Yasmine, they've arrived," she called over her shoulder. Turning back to the man dressed in a brown button down shirt and shorts, she said, *"Yes, we are expecting a delivery from On Call Publishing."*

"Okay, ma'am, I just need you to fill in your name and address here," he handed her an electronic device. *"And put your signature here,"* he said, pointing to a new screen. With the delivery accepted, he turned back to his truck.

Yasmine joined Lina in the doorway. She watched as the delivery man loaded five boxes onto a dolly and pulled it slowly up the steps that lead to the door. When he reached the top, he was drenched in sweat. Looking from Lina to Yasmine to the heavy boxes on the dolly, he asked, *"Would you like me to put them inside?"*

"Yes," Lina replied. *"That would be most helpful."* She moved aside to let the man pass. *"Just there in the corner is fine. Would you like some lemonade or water?"*

The delivery man wiped his forehead with the back of his arm. *"No thank you, ma'am. I have other deliveries waiting."*

When the delivery man had left, Yasmine ran to the desk to grab a pair of scissors. Lina peered over the boxes, looking at the address labels that bore her daughter's name. Yasmine stood up on tip toe to better see the top of the first box and began to cut the tape down the middle.

"No, no!" Lina stopped her.

"Why?" Yasmine asked surprised. *"Let's look at them now!"*

As much as Lina wanted to see the books as well, she pulled the scissors from Yasmine's hands, *"I think we should wait for your father to come."*

"But why?" Yasmine knew her mom was right, but she was desperate to see the books.

"*Your father has done quite a bit to make this a reality for you, and I think he should be here to see it with us when we open the boxes. I know he will want to share your joy. So we will wait,*" Lina said with finality.

"*AstaghfirUllaah, I am sorry, Mom. I was being greedy. We should wait for Dad,*" Yasmine apologized.

Lina looked at the clock and then stated, "*He will be home in just a few short hours. It will pass quickly.*"

But it didn't for Yasmine. She wandered the house with one eye constantly on the stack of boxes. Several times she picked up a novel to read only to put it down five minutes later because she couldn't concentrate. She cleaned her room and reorganized her files. As she cleaned out the milk crate containing her book research, she came across the fat folder of rejection letters. Yasmine briefly considered tossing the folder, but decided better of it. She would keep it as a reminder of the obstacles Allaah had helped her overcome.

Finally, she heard the front door close and her father's voice greeting her mother. Yasmine leaped down the stairs three at a time while yelling, "*Assalaamu-alaykum, Dad! Dad! Dad! Guess what came today?*"

Qadeer stood right next to the boxes. "*Hmmmm...let me see. You got a letter from your aunt, right?*" he teased Yasmine gently.

"*No, Dad!*" Yasmine was obviously not in the mood for teasing.

"*Well then, tell me, my love, what came today?*" Qadeer bent over to be eye level with Yasmine.

"*My books! My books came!*" Yasmine said pointing to the boxes.

"*Oh! Is that what all these boxes are for?*" Qadeer said with a twinkle in his eyes.

Lina laughed. "*Yasmine has been wearing holes in the carpet from walking circles around the living room, but we decided to wait for you to open and celebrate this big event.*" Yasmine nodded in agreement. "*So please put away your things and come back before Yasmine bounces through the ceiling.*"

Both parents looked at their daughter who was jumping up and down in place, giddy with anticipation. *"Okay, okay, I am going,"* Qadeer said, and he hurried to put away his briefcase.

Returning with the scissors, he handed them to Yasmine. *"Will you do the honors?"*

Yasmine's smile was so wide her parents were sure it would become permanently stuck in that position. She took the scissors and carefully cut open the tape on the top box. Then she took one last look at her name on the label before pulling up the flaps. Inside were neatly stacked copies of *Homeless No More*.

Pulling out the first book carefully, Yasmine walked to the couch and sat down. She ran her hand across the glossy front cover. The oversized paperback had a large photo of a happy family in their home with a smaller photo of a young child pulling a wagon down a desolate street in the upper corner. Yasmine traced her name which was printed under the title.

She felt surreal. Holding the book up to her nose, she flipped through and took in the scent of the new paper and binding. *Insha'Allaah*; that had been her prayer and her mother's prayer throughout this whole process, and surely it had been Allaah's (SWT) Will, since here she was sitting with her new book. Yasmine felt that someone must pinch her to make sure it was all real.

"Look here, Yasmine!" Lina stood in front of her, camera in hand. Yasmine held up the book and smiled brightly. "Say cheese!" The camera flashed brightly, and Lina looked at the small digital screen on the back of the camera.

"Let me see, Mom," Yasmine stood and walked to view the camera screen.

"We must always remember this day," Lina smiled brightly. She looked over at Qadeer, *"Today our little girl is also our little author."*

The next day, Lina drove around town to deliver copies of her books to all who had helped her. First was Mr. Barnes who was over the moon in delight. *"My first protégé,"* he had taken to telling anyone who would listen.

Then, the pair pulled up to the Guiding Light Shelter. Mrs. Wildey was expecting their visit and had cake and ice cream ready. With the staff, they had a small 'book release party' to celebrate Yasmine's achievement. Before they left, Yasmine left two copies of her book, one for Mrs. Wildey and one to be sent to the Governor's office.

Lina and Yasmine's final stop was Mr. Jenkins' bookstore. He took five copies for the store and placed one in the window.

"You should make up some flyers with order forms in case I run out," he told Yasmine.

Yasmine agreed to return with some later in the week. *"Can I maybe sign books here too sometime?"* she asked.

"You bet," Mr. Jenkins answered. *"When you come by with the flyers, bring your calendar, and we'll set a date."*

When Lina returned home, she found a message from Mrs. Wildey saying that Guiding Light Shelter would be sending out a press release about the book. A copy was being emailed to Lina for her review.

After listening to the message, Lina set down the phone and looked into the living room; there was Yasmine sitting on the couch writing. Lina smiled to herself and shook her head. Yasmine and her notebook – she was undoubtedly writing out an award-winning marketing strategy. Or maybe it was a sample of the flyer for Mr. Jenkins. Whatever it was, Lina was sure it would be great.

The next week was the start of school. Lina had been so excited by the book that she completely forgot about school. It wasn't until Qadeer reminded her that Yasmine would have to get up early to catch the bus the next day that she was brought back to reality. That was followed by a late night trip to the 24 hour supercenter to pick up school supplies.

In the morning, Yasmine was out of bed before anyone else. Qadeer found her waiting in the living room for *Fajr salaah*. Her backpack was sitting by her side, and she was curled up on the couch with a novel. His little girl was entering the fourth grade today.

After prayer, the family gathered for a hearty breakfast, and Yasmine ran out to the bus stop. Her backpack was heavy today. Not only did she have all her school supplies, but she had carefully tucked away two books. On the bus she stared out the window, paying particular attention to the homes that lined the street. *Insha'Allaah*, she prayed that every family could have a home like this.

"Hi, Mrs. Chrisman," Yasmine walked into the familiar kindergarten room.

"Hello, Yasmine," Mrs. Chrisman embraced her former student. "You are an author now!"

Yasmine smiled in return.

"I saw you in the paper," Mrs. Chrisman said. "What a lovely photo they had of you. You must be so proud!"

"I am very happy," Yasmine admitted, "but I am trying hard not to let it go to my head...that wouldn't please Allaah (SWT)."

Mrs. Chrisman nodded in agreement. Yasmine set down her backpack and opened it. She pulled out one of the two copies of the book she had packed this morning. She handed it to Mrs. Chrisman, "Here, I'd like you to have this."

"Oh, Yasmine," Mrs. Chrisman gasped. "How thoughtful of you." She admired the cover and then set it down on her desk. She pulled a pen out of the holder on her desk and uncapped it. "Of course, I would be honored if you would sign it so I could have an autographed copy."

"Of course, Mrs. Chrisman," Yasmine was happy to oblige.

At lunch, Yasmine found Sydney and gave her the other copy. Sydney flipped through it and then studied the back section which gave a short biography of Yasmine. "You'll be famous one day!" Sydney said. "And I'll be able to say that I knew you back when your first book came out!" Then the two friends laughed and giggled through lunch as Yasmine shared her many summer adventures.

The following month brought some normalcy back to Yasmine's life. She fell into the school routine again. Her day was marked by prayer, classes and her home studies. While not fluent, her Arabic skills were good enough to carry on a basic conversation. She had also started to move on to more advanced Islamic theology lessons at home.

But of all her home studies, the one she cherished the most was learning the Qur'aan. Originally, she hadn't been thrilled when her mom had insisted she learn it, but she had come to appreciate it now. It was comforting to have Allaah's (SWT) Word running through her mind as she went about her day. With more than half the Holy Book memorized, Yasmine was sure that she would have the entire Book memorized in a matter of a few short years.

The books sold at a steady rate of one or two each week. After the article in the paper, Yasmine received a flurry of orders and thought that she would surely sell out in no time. But it ended up being a temporary surge and now Yasmine sold mainly through Mr. Jenkins. He always kept a couple of the books on-hand and placed a flyer in every customer's bag.

In the evening after her home studies and dinner, she spent an hour or two each day working on how to market her business; she wrote up flyers and press releases or packed up the week's orders to be shipped.

In late October, Qadeer and Lina went to school for the fall teacher conference. As a fourth grader, Yasmine had graduated to having letter grades on her report card instead of the number system used in the younger grades. Lina had been worried that all the work on the book would affect Yasmine's grades, but she continued to excel in school.

The teacher had nothing but positive things to say about Yasmine, and the parents left the classroom in good spirits. Before leaving the building, they stopped to look at a bulletin board near the entrance.

"Excuse me," a voice said from behind.

Lina turned to see Yasmine's old kindergarten teacher. *"Why, Mrs. Chrisman, how nice to see you!"* Lina exclaimed.

Although Lina had not seen Mrs. Chrisman in quite some time, Yasmine talked about her often. She was well aware that Mrs. Chrisman had always been very supportive of Yasmine's many projects.

"It is good to see you too," Mrs. Chrisman said. *"I wanted to talk to you about Yasmine."*

Qadeer and Lina looked at one another. Mrs. Chrisman continued, *"I read her book and was most impressed. Your daughter is certainly bright and compassionate."* She paused and then said, *"I wanted to see if Yasmine could do an assembly for our students."*

"An assembly?" Qadeer asked.

"Yes, we regularly have guest speakers come and address the students. I thought Yasmine could do a presentation on how she became an author and then also talk about the homeless problem," Mrs. Chrisman looked from Lina to Qadeer.

"Oh, I don't know, Mrs. Chrisman," Lina said. *"Yasmine can be quite shy at times. I am not sure if she would want to give a talk in front of such a large group."*

"But maybe we should let Yasmine decide that," Qadeer suggested.

"Well, if it is all right with you, I will ask her about it tomorrow," Mrs. Chrisman offered.

"I just don't want Yasmine to feel pressured to do it...," Lina's voice trailed off.

"No pressure, I promise!" Mrs. Chrisman smiled.

The next morning, Mrs. Chrisman stopped by the lunch table where Yasmine and Sydney were sitting. "Yasmine, I was wondering if you would like to do a presentation for the school."

"What sort of presentation?" Yasmine asked.

"I was thinking that you could talk about how you decided to become an author and then you could also talk about the problem of homelessness," Mrs. Chrisman explained.

"I don't know...," Yasmine thought about the last school assembly. Everyone had been so rowdy that the teachers could hardly settle them down. Then half the school didn't seem to pay attention to the person talking.

"Do it!" Sydney nudged her. "It'll be cool!"

Yasmine gave a worried look. She couldn't even be called on in class without blushing. She would probably die from embarrassment in front of all those people. "But I wouldn't know what to say," she protested.

Mrs. Chrisman had anticipated that objection, "I can help. You could do a slide show presentation on the computer. We can put together the slides and they'll be projected onto a screen. If you get stuck, you can just read off the slides."

Yasmine still wasn't convinced. "Just think about it," Mrs. Chrisman said. "If you change your mind, let me know."

After she had gone, Sydney turned to her, "Why not?" she wanted to know.

"I could never stand up in front of the whole school. Anyway, I'd probably be boring and get booed off." Yasmine returned to her lunch.

Sydney picked up her sandwich too. "I'd do it," she shared. "I bet you'd sell a lot of books that way. It's like the people who go on talk shows to talk about their books."

Yasmine considered this and then pushed the thought out of her mind. She couldn't talk in front of a crowd like that; she simply couldn't.

It was only two days later that she changed her mind. Sydney's words kept coming back to her. This probably was a good way to sell some books. Maybe the kids wouldn't buy, but there were always parents who came to assemblies too. Mrs. Chrisman was thrilled to hear Yasmine's change of heart, and the two agreed to meet during recess in the computer lab to work on the presentation.

Yasmine felt a little funny talking about herself, but Mrs. Chrisman said that the students would be interested to know how she became a published author. So they started out the presentation with a few slides about Yasmine and the steps she took to write and later publish the book. This was followed by information about why people are homeless and, finally, what students could do to help. Mrs. Chrisman asked if Yasmine would want to answer questions at the end from the audience, but the young author flatly refused that suggestion.

Every night after dinner, Qadeer and Lina sat on the couch as Yasmine's captive audience. She gave her presentation, which ran for about half an hour, before them and wrote notes on anything that would need to be changed. It was not long before Yasmine had memorized the entire presentation and became comfortable even going off script when the mood struck her.

The assembly was scheduled for early December. On the big day, Qadeer planned to leave work early to attend the afternoon presentation. Yasmine's talk was scheduled as the last event for the day. She was excused from class half an hour early to head to the gym. Mrs. Chrisman was there as well.

Yasmine stood in the center of the gym while Mrs. Chrisman climbed the bleachers. Yasmine tested the microphone and adjustments were made to the volume. The computer was hooked up to the projector and tested as well.

In no time, throngs of students began pouring the gym. They jostled each other as they noisily pounded up the bleachers. Yasmine felt her confidence drain out of her; all those students; all those eyes that would be trained on her. She suddenly felt in a panic. She would surely make a fool of herself.

Mrs. Chrisman came over to retrieve the microphone so she could introduce Yasmine. *"I can't do it,"* Yasmine said when she approached.

"What?" Mrs. Chrisman whispered.

"I can't do it, Mrs. Chrisman, I'm sorry," Yasmine's eyes darted back and forth scanning the crowded gym.

Mrs. Chrisman crouched down to Yasmine's level. *"Yasmine, I know you're scared. You wouldn't be normal if you weren't. That's just part of talking to a group."* Yasmine's eyes returned to Mrs. Chrisman's, *"The important thing is to just imagine that you are back home practicing. Don't make eye contact with anyone, even friends – that will make you lose your concentration. Instead look at people's hair. Then it looks like you are looking at them. You can do this. I know you can."* Mrs. Chrisman bounced up without giving Yasmine a chance to reply.

Taking the microphone, the teacher turned to the crowd, *"Students, students,"* she said in a loud voice. *"If I can have your attention, please! We have a special presentation for you today..."*

Yasmine tuned out the rest of the conversation. She saw Sydney and gave her a small smile. Then her vision moved over her classmates and the other teachers. She saw Mrs. Richland and looked away quickly. In the corner of the bleachers, Lina and Qadeer were seated. Lina caught Yasmine's attention and gave her two thumbs up. Yasmine smiled tentatively.

Before she knew it, the students were clapping, and Mrs. Chrisman handed her the microphone. Showtime! Yasmine's stomach was in her throat and she was sure she would not be able to talk. Mrs. Chrisman walked to the computer and flipped the screen to the first slide. She gave Yasmine an encouraging smile, and Yasmine closed her eyes. She imagined herself back in her living room. Then she turned to the crowd and began to talk.

At first, Yasmine stuttered and tripped over her words. She was sure the laughter would start shortly, but it didn't. Some students were fidgety and staring at the ceiling, but most were paying attention. As she continued, she felt her confidence grow. By the end, she was talking freely without paying attention to the slides at all.

Surprising both Mrs. Chrisman and herself, she even spontaneously asked for questions at the end. Only a few hands went up including one kindergartener who wanted to know about Yasmine's *hijaab*. And then it was done.

Mrs. Chrisman gave a closing remark and dismissed the students back to the classroom. Several teachers and parents descended upon Yasmine. She was aware of people saying 'good job' and patting her on the back. The principal, Mr. Kelly, handed her a small bouquet of flowers in congratulations.

Over the shoulders of those surrounding her, Yasmine saw Mrs. Chrisman hurry to her parents. She said something to them, and Qadeer quickly disappeared through the door. He returned several minutes later carrying a box of Yasmine's books.

"Attention everyone," Mrs. Chrisman called to the parents and staff who were still milling about the gym. *"If anyone would like a copy of Yasmine's book we have copies available here."*

The crowd surrounding Yasmine left and walked towards Mrs. Chrisman. Seeing her opportunity, Lina walked up to Yasmine and embraced her tightly. *"Alhamdulillaah, my love, you did fantastic!"* She kissed Yasmine on the cheek and looked into her eyes. *"Who ever would have thought that Allaah (SWT) would do such great things with my daughter. I can barely believe that it was my little girl up there. You were so composed and gave such a great presentation."*

"I was so nervous, Mom," Yasmine confessed. *"I didn't think I was going to be able to talk at first."*

"But you never would have known, Yasmine," Lina told her. *"You looked completely comfortable while talking."*

"Thanks, Mom." Yasmine hugged her mom again and turned to look at the people who were busy buying her book.

Lina had just sat down for dinner when the telephone rang. Exasperated, she said to no one in particular, *"Who could be calling now?"*

Qadeer shrugged, and Yasmine looked down the hall to where the phone was, as if the answer lay down there. Lina balled up her napkin and tossed it next to her plate. With a huff, she walked to the hall.

Slightly annoyed, she answered, *"Assalaamu-alaykum? Yes, this is Yasmine's mother."* Then her tone softened. *"Why yes, we are very proud...yes...yes...that is very kind of you."* Yasmine looked at her father who appeared as confused as her.

Lina continued talking into the phone. *"Oh, heavens, no! She could do that for free...hmmm...you have a budget? Well, if you were planning on it...okay, let me get a paper here."* Lina grabbed a pen from the desk and began scribbling on the back of an envelope. Then she hung up the phone.

Hurrying back to the table, Lina shared the good news. *"That was a teacher from Apple Ridge School."*

"Apple Ridge? Across town?" Qadeer inquired.

"Yes," Lina went on, *"it sounds like a parent from our school was telling a parent from their school about Yasmine's presentation. That parent suggested to their principal that Yasmine come and speak there. That was the teacher who coordinates their assemblies."*

Yasmine's mind quickly began to calculate how many books she could sell at Apple Ridge. She had sold nearly 20 at her school assembly, but Apple Ridge was a lot bigger.

Lina's voice brought her focus back to the table, *"But that is not the best part."* She paused for effect.

"So tell us the best part, Lina," Qadeer prompted her.

"The best part is that they have a budget for assemblies. They will pay our Yasmine $200 to speak to the school."

Yasmine dropped her fork. *"They'll pay me to talk?"* she asked amazed.

Lina nodded. *"I told them you would do it for free, but the teacher wouldn't hear of it. She said that they had $200 to pay whoever they found as a speaker."*

"Wow!" Yasmine mouthed to her father.

"Wow is right," Qadeer agreed. *"There is no doubt Allaahu Akbar."*

Chapter 10

Yasmine's Presentation

After the presentation at Apple Ridge, another article appeared in the paper. One of the Apple Ridge parents was a reporter for the local paper. He took a photo of Yasmine speaking and interviewed her afterwards.

Qadeer bought several copies of the paper and brought them home. Lina clipped the copies and addressed letters to several relatives to share the good news. Yasmine took one copy and carefully placed it in a scrapbook she had begun with her press clippings. As she placed in the new clipping, she stopped to look at the newsletter clipping from the Guiding Light Shelter. She said a prayer of thanksgiving and asked for Allaah's (SWT) protection for the Shelter and all who took refuge there.

The news article had the snowball effect of leading to new speaking engagements. Yasmine was soon booked at schools throughout the county. She lengthened her presentation to nearly an hour, and schools began paying $500 for her to speak. And it wasn't just schools who were interested in Yasmine's message; she was the featured presenter for the Rotary Club once a week and at a government conference as well.

Lina was worried about the effect of the presentations on Yasmine's school work. She was still maintaining her grades, but Lina could see the weariness in her eyes. She was missing almost a full day of school each week and spent many nights working long hours to make up the work she had missed.

Confiding in her husband, Lina told Qadeer, *"I don't think this is a healthy schedule for Yasmine."*

Qadeer nodded but did not respond.

"It's not that I don't want her to excel," Lina continued, *"but it doesn't seem right for a 10 year old to work so hard."*

Qadeer nodded again, *"It is April now? And school is over in a month and a half?"* He considered this. *"I think we should not schedule anything else until the end of the school year."* Lina began to protest, but he stopped her, *"I don't mean that we should cancel what is already scheduled – just do not schedule anything else."*

Lina agreed. *"And for next year?"* she asked.

"Next year is fifth grade. Classes will be harder. I think that Yasmine is making enough money that she would be able to hire a tutor if she'd like. Or if she doesn't want to leave school, we will have to limit the amount of speaking engagements she can accept

in the fall." Qadeer looked at Lina, *"But I think she should make that decision."*

Qadeer called Yasmine down from her room and explained their concerns. He offered her the two options. *"I don't know,"* Yasmine responded. She did not want to give up her speaking. Now that she had experienced it, she discovered that she loved giving talks and sharing with others. On the other hand, she thought about Sydney and how much she would miss her.

"Think about it," Lina said. *"You don't have to decide now. You still have a month and a half of this school year plus the summer to decide."*

Yasmine agonized over the decision for weeks until a new development made it easy. The number of media and speaking requests had blossomed to such a point that Lina and Qadeer set up a separate phone line just for Yasmine's business. That phone was in the den where the door could be closed so the ringing phone would not disturb the family.

Lina had been so used to hearing the phone ring from the den that she was surprised one evening to hear instead a call coming in on the old phone line in the hall. Qadeer was closest to the phone and answered it. He listened for a moment and then said, *"Let me have you talk to my wife. She has been coordinating all of Yasmine's activities."* He held out the phone to Lina.

Perplexed, she stood up and took it from him. *"Hello? Oh, hi, how nice to hear from you...yes, Yasmine talks about her all the time. I think they are as tight as can be...uh huh...yes...oh, I don't think that will be necessary...if you insist...so Mondays in the afternoon once school gets out? Alright, yes...well, thank you for the call."*

Now Yasmine was confused, *"What was all that about?"*

Lina sat back down on the couch, *"That was Sydney's mom."*

Sydney's Mom? Yasmine wondered what she could want.

Answering the question that Yasmine had not actually said aloud, Lina shared, *"She wanted to know if you would coach Sydney."*

"Coach? Coach what?" Yasmine's mom should know that she didn't play sports.

"Coach as in help her start her own business," Lina informed her.

"Oh," Yasmine said.

"It sounds like Sydney has been talking up a storm about you at her home. Her mom says that she really wants to start a business like you, but doesn't know where to begin."

Yasmine thought for a moment, *"I'm not sure how to coach someone like that."*

"And you didn't know how to give a presentation either until you tried," Qadeer reminded her.

Yasmine shook her head. She still wasn't sure. Lina added, "Sydney's mom said she'll pay you $20 each week if you'll come each Monday and spend a couple hours with Sydney during the summer.

This Yasmine could not believe, *"She wants to pay me to hang out with my friend?"* She exclaimed, *"I'd go there every week for free."*

Lina patted her leg, *"I know you would dear, but you also have to be realistic. You make a lot of money speaking now. Your skills are worth something, and Sydney's mom knows it. If she didn't pay you something, she feels like she would be taking advantage of you."*

"If you say so, Mom."

With that decided the matter of whether to stay in school for fifth grade was almost a moot point. Sydney had been the one factor that would have swayed Yasmine to cut down on her speaking to stay in the classroom. But now that she would see Sydney each week for coaching, she agreed to hire a tutor instead.

Lina spent long hours researching tutoring programs and talked to countless individuals on the phone to find references and personal recommendations from others. When she had narrowed the search down to three individuals, Qadeer took the day off work to interview each one.

In the end they settled on Miss Amira Razak; a young Muslim woman with no family nearby, Lina felt that the tutoring arrangement would be mutually beneficial. Amira had confided during the interview that she felt somewhat isolated since most of those she worked with were not Muslim and did not understand her faith. But beyond that, she was a competent teacher with impeccable credentials and teaching ability.

When Lina introduced Amira to Yasmine, the two instantly hit it off. They chatted like old friends, and Lina felt that without a doubt she had made the right decision.

Summer came and Yasmine began to coach Sydney each week. Her speaking engagements slowed as schools let out but community organizations continued to call. Then one day a letter arrived. The return address was from France. Yasmine was at Sydney's house so Lina set the letter aside for later, but she continued to wrack her brain about who could be writing from France.

When it was time to pick up Yasmine, she placed the letter in her purse. After Yasmine had hopped in the car and buckled up, Lina handed her the envelope, *"This arrived today."*

Yasmine flipped it over and studied the return address. Then she slit the top of the envelope open. A check fell into her lap as she opened the letter. Yasmine picked up the check and her eyes went wide. *"Wow!"* she gasped.

"What is it?" Lina asked. Yasmine didn't answer right away. Lina said again, *"Yasmine, what is it?"*

"It's a lot of money – that's what!"

Lina couldn't contain her curiosity any longer. She pulled over into the parking lot of a store they were passing. Yasmine set down the check and picked up the letter.

Looking at the check, Lina's eyes went as wide as Yasmine's had been. Yasmine said excitedly, *"It's from Omar Sharif! He answered my letter."* Yasmine read from the correspondence:

Dear Yasmine,

Thank you for your letter. You seem like an extraordinary young girl.

I would like to help you with your quest to publish your book. Enclosed is a check to help with the cost of printing. I hope it will be enough. And in case it is too much, please do with the remainder what you feel Allaah (SWT) is leading you to do.

Alhamdulillaah,

Omar Sharif

The check was for $5,000. Lina looked from the check to Yasmine. Her daughter met her eyes, *"What should we do, Mom? I already published the book?"*

"Well," Lina suggested, *"he says you should do what Allaah (SWT) leads you to do. What is your heart telling you?"*

Yasmine didn't even have to think, *"The money should go to the Guiding Light Shelter."*

Lina nodded, *"That is an excellent idea. Now, let's hurry home so we can email Mrs. Wildey with the good news."*

Mrs. Wildey was a master at maximizing press coverage so the presentation of Omar Sharif's money was no simple affair. She contacted his representatives by phone and discussed the situation. While Mr. Sharif could not attend in person, he mailed greetings to be read at the check presentation.

Yasmine was center-stage at what could best be described as a media circus. All three news stations, the local paper and two radio stations tried to cram into the tiny shelter office. The girl who made the donation possible gave a few remarks followed by Mrs. Wildey. Cameras flashed and supporters cheered.

Of course, the event was followed by more media coverage and the sale of more of Yasmine's books. She was down to the last few books in the last box now.

Lina and Yasmine had spent many days discussing whether to publish more and how many to order. But again, Allaah (SWT) helped make the decision easy.

"Hello? Lina?" the voice on the other end of the phone asked.

"Yes," Lina answered.

"This is Mr. Barnes."

"Oh, yes, we haven't heard from you in a while. How are you?"

"Very well, thank you. I wanted to see how many of Yasmine's books you have left."

"Only a few – we've actually been discussing whether to buy more."

"But you haven't yet?"

"No."

"Good. Because I sent a copy to my editor who shared it with a colleague at another firm; I received a call this morning from that woman, and she'd like to do the second run."

"Really?"

"Really."

"Oh, how fabulous!" Lina motioned for Yasmine to come over near the phone.

"I'll bring the paperwork with me to the next Rotary Club meeting. Will Qadeer and Yasmine be there?"

"Yes, they will. Thank you so much!"

And with that Mr. Barnes and Lina said their good-byes. Putting down the phone, Lina turned to Yasmine. *"We don't have to order any more books from On Call Publishing! A regular publishing house is going to buy the book from you!"*

Yasmine jumped into the air, *"Whoohoo!"* she cried out.

The editor, Maxine Reynolds, flew out to meet Yasmine shortly thereafter. She was a no-nonsense woman with short spiky hair. Her curt tone and manner made Yasmine think that she didn't like her. Mr. Barnes later explained that many editors were like that, and it was nothing personal.

She drew up the paperwork which Qadeer reviewed carefully. Mr. Barnes had also arranged for his attorney to be present to review all the documents. Once those were signed, Mrs. Reynolds rattled off at a clipped pace all that would take place. New cover art would be designed, and the book would be issued as a hardcover edition. The publisher would send out copies to various newspapers and magazines and arrange interviews. Finally, there were plans for a regional book tour to kick-off the publication.

"Oh my," Lina said. *"That's so much. Is it all necessary?"*

"Absolutely," Mrs. Reynolds said abruptly. *"Promotion, promotion, promotion; it's the way to sell books."*

With the papers signed and the plans in order, Mrs. Reynolds left as quickly as she arrived.

Through the remainder of the summer, Lina made every effort to ensure that Yasmine had plenty of time to rest and relax. She had no doubt that Yasmine was enjoying all her success, but Lina wanted to make it a priority that she also enjoyed being a child. After all, despite all she had been through, she was still just a 10 year old child.

One day, after spending a leisurely morning reading, Yasmine approached her mother. *"Mom, can we talk?"*

"Of course," Lina put down her magazine and turned to Yasmine who sat beside her on the couch.

"I have a lot of money in the bank," Yasmine stated matter-of-factly.

"You know you do," Lina said. Qadeer and Lina always kept it foremost in their mind that money Yasmine earned was Yasmine's money. She still had her original bank accounts and access to her checking. When it came time for taxes, Qadeer always carefully explained to her how much she was earning and how much needed to go to the government.

Despite this, Yasmine had never seemed overly concerned with her money. She continued to send a monthly *sadaqah* to the Guiding Light Shelter and occasionally she would buy herself books or treat Sydney to a movie. Now, she said simply, *"I'd really like to get my cat now."*

This took Lina by surprise. *"Oh,"* she thought with a bittersweet feeling of how Yasmine's world used to revolve around cats. Before the book, cats were all she would talk about. It had been quite a while since the subject had come up. Lina scolded herself again for failing to remember her daughter was just a child; so many of their conversations revolved around adult issues and business. Lina told herself that she needed to do a better job of not always being so serious. *AstaghfirUllaah.*

"Is that okay?" Yasmine broke her mom's trance.

"Oh," Lina looked up startled. *"Yes, of course."* She smiled at Yasmine and touched her cheek. *"It's just that I haven't heard you mention cats in such a long time. Do you still want the American Bobtail?"*

Yasmine shook her head, *"No…I mean yes, but I want to get a cat from the shelter. The American Bobtails that breeders sell will probably find a good home, but the ones at the shelter are homeless. I want to help one that is homeless."*

"That's my beautiful, caring girl. When do you want to go?"

"Can we go today?"

"I don't see why not. Let's wait until after our noon prayer."

Yasmine's bright, girlish smile spread across her face. *"Thanks, Mom!"*

The shelter was a stark building with cinder block walls. The sound of barking echoed from the distance. When Lina and Yasmine entered, a woman behind the counter looked up, *"Are you here to find a lost dog?"*

"No," Lina answered. *"We are looking for a cat."*

"For a lost cat, I need you to fill out this form," the woman dropped a clipboard on the counter.

Yasmine stepped up, "Not a lost cat. We want to adopt a cat."

"Oh," the woman grabbed the clipboard back. "Go through those doors and turn left. Cats are down at the end. If you find one you like, take the card from its kennel and bring it back here."

Lina led the way and Yasmine followed down the hall. Through the door, the sound of barking became deafening. Yasmine put her hands to her ears as she made her way down to the cat section. Off the hallway were a series of doors. Each door led to a new hallway lined with cages.

Stopping in front of the first door marked 'cats', Lina said, "I guess we start here."

Going through the rooms one by one, Yasmine looked intently at each animal. Some ran to the door meowing while others lingered in the back of their cage. A few hissed at Yasmine when she peered through the bars. In the final room were two large kennels filled with kittens. They squawked loudly when they saw Yasmine.

"Oh how sad," Lina commented. Yasmine looked up at her, "all these babies without their mothers."

Yasmine crouched near the floor and ran her fingers by the bars. The kittens rubbed up against the cage asking to be petted. Yasmine spotted a small black and white cat near the back of the crowded cage. It tried once and then twice to make its way to the front, but each time was pushed back by its rowdy cage-mates.

"I want that one," Yasmine said pointing to the black and white kitten.

"Are you sure?" Lina asked.

Yasmine nodded and stood to find the card for the kitten. However, there were none by the cage. Lina and Yasmine walked back to the front desk to ask about the kitten.

"Oh, we have so many kittens, we don't keep cards on them," the woman at the desk said. She pulled out a few sheets of paper and attached them to a clipboard. "I need you to fill this out and then we can go get it for you." Yasmine took the clipboard. "Actually," the woman corrected, "I need your mom to fill it out. Minors can't adopt animals."

Yasmine handed the clipboard to Lina who filled it out. When that was finished, Yasmine paid the adoption fee and the woman grabbed a set of keys from the wall. Together, the trio walked to the last door and entered the room with the kittens.

"Okay, which one do you want?" the woman asked.

Yasmine pointed to the black and white one, and the cage was unlocked. Instantly, a sea of kittens came pouring out the front of the kennel. The woman knocked them back with her leg and grabbed the kitten in question. It let out a yelp as she lifted it in one hand. The door of the cage swung shut and the other kittens meowed in despair.

The woman handed the kitten to Yasmine who cradled it in her arms. Its small body quivered slightly and then sank against Yasmine. She petted it softly and a small purr rose from the kitten's body.

Back in the car, Yasmine squinted to see through the holes in the box the kitten had been placed in for the ride home. Its small pathetic sounding meow came from a corner of the box. *"I think it's scared,"* Yasmine observed.

"You probably would be too if someone yanked you out of a cage and put you in a box," Lina commented. *"Oh, dear,"* she said as she started up the car.

"What, Mom?" asked Yasmine.

"We weren't thinking," Lina said. *"We forgot all about food and litter and everything else we'll need."*

"We can just stop on the way home," Yasmine suggested.

Lina shook her head. *"It is far too warm a day to leave a kitten in the car while we shop. It would roast."*

Both Lina and Yasmine thought for a moment. Then Yasmine said, *"Sydney says that she takes her dog to the pet store on Division Street. If they let dogs go, they will probably let cats."*

"Good idea!" Lina added with a flourish, *"Off we go!"*

The pet store did allow animals of all types so the kitten was a welcome guest. Lina and Yasmine walked the aisles picking up supplies while the box in their cart continued to meow its sad cry.

At home, Yasmine and Lina decided on the location of the litter box and the food dish. Then, Yasmine opened the box and carefully took out the kitten. She showed the kitten her food dish where it promptly ate everything. The next stop was a visit to the litter box before going back to the living room. Yasmine lay on the floor next to the kitten dangling toys over its head. She giggled and laughed as it fell backwards and rolled on the floor.

Qadeer opened the door, surprised to see Yasmine and her new pet. *"Assalaamu-alaykum, Dad,"* she exclaimed. *"This is my cat, Amber!"*

Chapter 11

The Feeling of Productivity

When September came, Yasmine felt strange staying home. She peered out the window to look at the other students walking down their street. They were wearing their new clothes and had stiff backpacks filled with supplies. Although Yasmine was happy knowing that she would be able to continue her speaking engagements, she felt a twinge of sadness too. There would be no early morning rendezvous with Mrs. Chrisman to see how her summer went. No nervous excitement of meeting her teacher for the first time and learning who her new classmates would be. No giggling with Sydney at lunch time.

Turning away from the window, she sat on the couch and flipped through a copy of the magazine, *Sisters* lying on the end table. She stopped on an article reflecting on how Muslim women could connect with Allaah on a daily basis. The doorbell rang, and she looked up.

Lina walked to the door and opened it. *"Amira! Welcome, welcome. Come in."*

Yasmine set the magazine down. *"Assalaamu-alaykum, Amira,"* she called from the couch.

"Hello, how are you doing this morning?" Amira asked.

"Good," Yasmine answered.

"All right," Lina clapped her hands. *"Why don't you two go to the kitchen table and get started."*

Lina and Qadeer had spent a great deal of time with Amira over the summer reviewing Yasmine's curriculum. Since her learning could be completely customized, Lina had asked to incorporate the Qur'aan, Arabic and Islamic studies as part of the tutoring. Amira was fluent in Arabic and had taken college courses in Islamic studies so she was happy to oblige.

Amira began to unpack several papers and books from her bag. *"Today, we will start with some evaluations,"* she explained. *"Your mother and father have filled me in about what you have learned before, but I have a series of sheets and exams to let me know exactly what your strengths are and where you might need some extra help."*

Yasmine sat down and began the series of quizzes and tests that Amira had prepared. It was a long and tedious day, but Amira promised that every day wouldn't be that way. Lina prepared lunch and the trio stopped to eat followed by noon prayers. Then a couple more hours of work followed before Amira packed up her papers and left. The textbooks were left behind for Yasmine to store in the hall desk.

With the second printing of Yasmine's book coming near, Lina often spent her evenings talking to Mrs. Reynolds and mapping out the book tour on her calendar. The tour would take Yasmine through five states and require her to be on the road for nearly a month.

It was agreed that not only Lina, but also Amira would join Yasmine on the tour. Lina insisted on no more than three signings in any given week to ensure plenty of downtime and to allow for a more leisurely travel pace. The publisher was making all the arrangements and would pay for the travel and hotel accommodations.

In early January, Yasmine hit the road with her two chaperones. They travelled from city to city changing hotel rooms on nearly a nightly basis. Lina had been worried that the experience would wear on Yasmine, but she seemed to thrive on the attention.

At each book signing, she was allowed a short period to speak to whomever might be in the store and then she sat at a table for several hours to sign books. Sometimes 3 people showed up and sometimes 30. With the exception of just a few cranky customers, almost everyone was nice and interested in what Yasmine had to say. Lina marveled at her daughter's ability to win over a crowd. Even customers, who didn't know the book signing was going on, came over to chat with Yasmine and eventually left with her book.

Mrs. Reynolds met the group at one stop to see how the tour was progressing. She smiled approvingly as Yasmine gave her speech and chatted with audience members, young and old, afterwards. *"Your daughter has a real gift,"* she told Lina.

Lina nodded in agreement, *"If you had told me just two years ago that she could do this, I would never have believed it. She used to be so shy!"*

No matter where Yasmine, Lina and Amira might be, they always paused five times a day to pray. If possible, Lina tried to visit the mosque in the city where they stayed so Yasmine could see that Islam was something shared by people across the country.

Either in the morning or the night, Amira always claimed at least two hours to study with Yasmine. She had become attached to her young charge and was not about to let travel stand in the way of academics. Sometimes, while traveling on the bus that carried them from stop to stop, she would quiz Yasmine. Other times she insisted on speaking Arabic to sharpen her student's skills.

One evening, Yasmine and Amira sat at the small table set in the corner of their hotel room. Amira was explaining the rules of division as they applied to fractions and decimals. The phone rang in the bedroom where Yasmine could hear her mother answer. There was a murmur of quiet talking and then Lina entered the front room of the small suite.

"Alhamdulillaah, a new opportunity for you, Yasmine," she announced.

"What?" both Yasmine and Amira asked at once.

"That was your father." Yasmine missed her father terribly. He called most nights, but it simply wasn't the same. She missed his gentle voice and his hearty laugh. Inwardly she sighed at the thought that her mom had not called her to the phone to talk to him.

"And what was his news?" Amira picked up the conversation.

"He received a call today from a Homeless Coalition based in Washington D.C.," Lina said. "They are having their annual conference and would like Yasmine to run one of their break-out sessions."

Yasmine returned to the conversation, "A break-out session?"

"A break-out session is a smaller group at a convention," Amira explained. "You see, everyone gets together for breakfast or lunch or the featured speaker and then they 'break out' into smaller groups for the rest of the conference. That way they have different choices about what to learn about."

"Oh, sounds complicated," Yasmine responded.

"It's not really," Lina added. "You can just do a shortened version of your presentation. There will be another presenter in the session too, and then you can both answer questions from the audience."

"I see," that did seem a lot like what Yasmine already did for her speaking engagements. It was just that someone else would be with her this time.

Lina sat at the table. "The only thing is we'll have to go straight from the book tour to Washington D.C. for the conference."

Yasmine thought for a moment; she desperately wanted to see her dad for a while and sleep in her own bed.

Sensing her apprehension, Lina commented, *"I know it's been a long trip. If you want to go home, I understand. But on the bright side, they'll pay you $1,000 to attend."*

That settled it for Yasmine. *"In that case, let's go,"* she said with a smile. No one had ever paid her $1,000 before. She could handle a couple more days on the road for that much money.

Washington D.C. was still drab and cold. The gray snow had clung to the curbs along the roadways. Still, there was a special grace about the city. The Washington Monument gleamed in the sun and seemed to stand guard over the memorials and statues that dotted the landscape.

Yasmine arrived in Washington D.C. two days before the conference was scheduled to start. Not one to miss an educational opportunity, Amira made sure that Yasmine saw all the sites. *"We'll focus on American history and government for the next few days,"* she said.

So Yasmine and Lina followed Amira to the Arlington Cemetery and saw the tomb of the Unknown Solider, the memorial of the Challenger Astronauts, and the final resting place of JFK. They stopped by the memorial of Iwo Jima where Amira discussed the Asian arena battles of World War II followed by the Vietnam Memorial where Yasmine learned about that conflict. Then there were trips to the presidential monuments, Mount Vernon and a drive-by of the White House.

It was an exhausting two days. Lina felt that she had learned as much as Yasmine during this time. But when Amira suggested touring the Capitol, Lina had to say no more; on another trip she suggested, for the next day would be the start of the conference, and Yasmine must get to bed early.

Normally, Yasmine protested her mother's attempts to set an early bedtime, but not on this day. She was asleep in the rental car before they even arrived at the hotel. Lina gently rustled her awake and led her inside. Once tucked into her bed, Lina gave her daughter a gentle kiss and said an extra dua for Allaah's (SWT) guidance and protection for the next day.

The conference was the biggest event Yasmine had ever spoken at. She arrived early with her program on a computer flash drive. The event coordinator gave her a small gift basket in thanks for her attendance. Yasmine was amazed that not only was she being paid to talk, but she was receiving gifts as well.

She was shown the room where her presentation would take place and instructed to arrive 15 minutes before her scheduled time. She would give the presentation once in the morning and once in the evening. Lina and Yasmine then joined the attendees in the main conference room for a breakfast and to hear the opening comments.

When it was time to leave, Yasmine and Lina excused themselves and walked to the smaller room where the other presenter was already waiting.

"Hello," he said extending his hand.

"Hello," Yasmine said shyly shaking hands.

"My name is Max Burton. I am the Executive Director of a consortium of homeless shelters here in the D.C. area, and you must be the Yasmine I've heard so much about."

"I'm Yasmine," she replied.

Mr. Burton continued, "You certainly are making waves within the homeless advocacy community. Everyone is talking about what life you've breathed in our cause."

Yasmine blushed fiercely, and Lina interjected, "You are too kind Mr. Burton. Yasmine is simply following her heart."

"Well, I wish more kids nowadays would do that," Mr. Burton said.

The room began to fill with conference attendees. Many carried coffee and a few had brought pastries from breakfast. They filled in the seats and tables throughout the room. Then a conference organizer introduced both Yasmine and Mr. Burton. With confidence, Yasmine stepped forwards and faced the crowd. Remembering the advice first given by Mrs. Chrisman, she focused on their hair instead of their eyes. And then she began.

At the end of the conference, everyone in attendance had to fill out a survey of their experience. Yasmine later learned that her presentation received some of the highest marks of the conference. Alhamdulillaah, Yasmine reminded herself. All the praise belonged to Allaah (SWT) alone. Yasmine was only His humble servant.

Throughout the next year, Yasmine spoke at numerous conferences around the country. The $1,000 speaking fee became the norm, and Lina, Amira and Yasmine crisscrossed the country.

Depending on what the conference offered, they would either ride in a plane or take a bus. Occasionally, they even traveled by train.

Magazines such as *Times, U.S. News, World Report, Emel, American Girl* and *Inc* highlighted Yasmine's accomplishments. She began to write her second book, a story about Muslims living in the United States and the challenges she faced. Since her unfortunate run-in with Mrs. Richland years before, it had been an issue that was close to her heart.

Many nights, Yasmine lay in bed praising Allaah. Her whole life had become surreal. She could not believe that all this was happening to her. Surely, it was a dream from which she would wake at any moment.

The following March, Yasmine had just turned 13 years old. Although she should technically be finishing up her sixth grade studies, she was actually moving on to high school courses. Between her natural aptitude and Amira's superior teaching skills, Yasmine had thrived through the tutoring arrangement.

She was sitting at the kitchen table reviewing the day's lessons when she heard her father calling from the den.

"Lina! Yasmine! Come here!" His voice carried through the whole house.

Lina walked down the stairs from where she had been folding laundry. *"Was that your father?"* she asked.

"Sounded like it," Yasmine replied while walking towards the den. Qadeer had spent the last week working overtime. Taxes were nearly due and as an accountant this was his busiest time of year.

Tonight, his goal had been to finish up his own tax return and Yasmine's as well. Lina and Yasmine walked into the den. *"What is it, Qadeer?"* Lina asked.

"Come here," he motioned urgently for them to walk around the desk.

"What?" Lina asked again.

"I finished Yasmine's tax return. Look here," he turned the computer monitor and pointed to a figure.

Yasmine had seen the tax forms before but wasn't sure exactly what she was looking at. She looked from her dad to her mom.

Lina's eyes widened as she comprehended exactly what she was seeing. *"Oh Yasmine!"* she exclaimed. *Alhamdulillaah, you are a millionaire!"*

Epilogue

Yasmine fidgeted in her seat. She bounced her knee slightly and leaned over to look past the people standing there.

"Where is he?" she asked.

"He is coming," Lina assured her. *"Be patient."*

"But he'll miss it," Yasmine insisted.

"Oh don't be silly," Lina said. *"He won't miss anything."*

And then there he was. Qadeer moved through the crowd jostling the three sandwiches in his hand. He arrived with a smile and handed one to each of the women sitting there.

And Yasmine was certainly now a young woman. At 14 years old, she had grown tall and slender. She carried herself with a graceful confidence that Lina found herself envying.

Lina marveled at the person beside her who had once been her baby. Well, she would always be my baby Lina thought; to others she might be a speaker and an author, but to me, she will always be my darling child.

A few weeks earlier, Yasmine had demonstrated her competence in reciting the Qur'aan. At her tender age, she had fully memorized all of Allaah's (SWT) Word. She was a woman full of not only grace but also wisdom. But she is still a child, Lina reminded herself. As if sensing her mother's thoughts, Yasmine let out a small whine, *"I hope Amber will be okay."*

"Why wouldn't Amber be okay?" Qadeer asked.

"Because this is the longest she'll ever have been away from all three of us, that's why," Yasmine explained. Sometimes, her dad just didn't get it.

"I am sure that Sydney will take good care of your cat," Lina assured her.

"Yes," Qadeer added, *"We will probably get home and Amber will insist on staying with Sydney."*

"Dad!" Yasmine groaned.

Qadeer laughed. *"No, I am quite sure that your cat, Amber will be waiting desperate for your return. I hear Sydney has a big* dog. No cat would choose to live with a dog when they can stay someplace dog-free."

"And you know this because you have such great insight into the thoughts of cats, right?" Lina gently chided her husband.

Yasmine laughed and then looked around. Nervous energy coursed through her body. Worse than anytime she spoke in front of a crowd. The airport terminal was packed with people milling about. People like them; people just trying to pass the time.

She wished she could hurry up the process. She didn't know why they had to get there so early. It seemed like everything with planes was hurry up and then wait. Not only that, but Qadeer had insisted that they arrive especially early to make their way through traffic. In hindsight this had been a good idea. Lina and Yasmine passed through security with little problem, but Qadeer had been pulled to the side so his luggage could be searched. The security guard asked him numerous questions and then called his supervisor who arrived to ask the same questions over again.

It was a scenario Yasmine has seen time and time again, but she became tired of it. She understood the need for safety, but it was frustrating that her family automatically became suspect because of the way they looked.

After the security guard and his supervisor had been satisfied by Qadeer's answers they let him pass. Lina knew the questions were probably just a ruse; a way to buy time while Qadeer's identity was passed through a database of questionable individuals. However, Lina knew her husband to be an upright man of righteous convictions. There was nothing to fear and the security stop was nothing more than an inconvenience and annoyance.

Now at the gate on the concourse, the family had nothing to do but wait. Yasmine had packed a book in her carry-on luggage, but was too excited to think of reading. She could see the plane waiting to be loaded.

"Why don't they let us on?" she asked impatiently.

"Because the flight does not leave for some time," Lina answered. "It is better to wait here than in cramped airplane seats. You've flown enough to know that, Yasmine."

"I know, Mom. I just wish we could go," Yasmine sighed.

"We all do," Qadeer stated. "This trip is such a blessing to us. We are all anxious to start the journey."

Finally, the airline attendant began the boarding procedure. When it was their turn, Yasmine, Lina and Qadeer picked up their bags and proceeded to the plane.

Their Hajj to Makkah had begun.

Have You Booked "The Most Inspirational Muslim Woman Speaker In America"?

Zohra Sarwari

The Ideal Professional Speaker for Your Next Event!

"Zohra Sarwari has stood out as exceptionally creative and extraordinarily passionate about her topics. Her energy is contagious."
Muhammad Alshareef
President, AlMaghrib Institute

"Zohra Sarwari has a great skill for making you want to achieve on a higher level. Your students will enjoy learning from her!"
Jonathan Sprinkles
Former APCA National College 'Speaker of the Year'
www.jsprinkles.com

"After hearing Zohra Sarwari's speech, I was profoundly moved by her enthusiasm to further educate me on the way the Muslim's live. Her knowledge instilled a greater understanding and appreciation in me."
Debbie Burke
High School Teacher
Indianapolis, Indiana

"Zohra Sarwari was very engaging and successfully captivated her audience. She was able to present visuals and demonstrated knowledge of her materials. At the end she was encircled by students who wanted to talk to her and purchase her books."
Catherine Rue
Student Life Administrator
Northampton Community College (Bethlehem, PA)

"Zohra is one of the most relevant speakers I have ever heard. She takes a very serious topic and makes it easy to understand. The information Zohra provides is very timely and purposeful. I am sure your audience will appreciate her approach and effective delivery. Thanks for shedding some light on my world as well."

Stan Pearson II, MBA
Author - Speaker - Radio Personality

"This interview had a great balance of information and passion for that information. Despite the indignities (to put it mildly) that Zohra has experienced, she came through positive and upbeat. May I be so lucky that all my interviews are like this."

Tom Berryman
Voices of the Tri-States, KDTH
Voted the number One public affairs program two years running by the Iowa Broadcast News Association.

"Zohra's effort should be viewed in two disciplines. The first discipline is that we seek a destiny that befits our quality of life. The second discipline is that we seek a destiny to befit the quality of earning in our lives. She has carefully crafted a dialogue of addressing our spiritual, emotional, and financial roadblocks. This book is a win-win for those don't win enough, and for those who may not have won at all. Embrace the book, begin your journey."

Preacher Moss
Founder of "Allah Made me Funny"
The Official Muslim Comedy Tour

'9 Steps To Achieve Your Destiny'
Do your best and let the Creator take care of the rest!

'9 Steps To Achieve Your Destiny' *explores the steps that, if practiced daily, will change your life God-willing. It shows you how your thinking and habits can either make you successful or stagnant, and helps you navigate your way to the right choices and productive habits. At times each of us may find ourselves lost in the darkness, searching for answers. This book will guide you to the light and help you stay there.* **'9 Steps To Achieve Your Destiny'** *will open your eyes to your own untapped strengths that can steer you to personal success. Seeking knowledge is the key. Let the journey begin!*

"Zohra Sarwari's book is remarkable because it is geared towards not only youth but all age groups. Anyone who reads this book will take away a valuable lesson filled with inspiration. This book shows us that it does not matter who you are or what your circumstance is, your success lies within you and this book has inspired me to continue with my dreams and turn them into actual goals and pursue them. It doesn't just leave you motivated with no direction, but provides you with actual steps on how to improve yourself and how to achieve your goals with Islamic motivation, something that is lacking these days."
Maida Besic

'Imagine that Today is Your Last Day'
How would you act if you knew that today was the last day of your life?

Death is somewhere near you and you can be its next victim. Do you know when you will die? No! Are you prepared for this inevitable journey? Probably not! Learn the tactics to make the most of your life thus preparing you for your death, and life in the hereafter. InshAllaah- God willing.

Imagine that Today is Your Last Day *reveals to you the secrets of living a great life and accepting your fate when it arrives. The book discusses the missing link in your life for which you will have to pay a price after death. Bring every moment to life, it can be your LAST day TODAY! It is an experience that many never think about, let alone go through it.*

This book will inspire and motivate you to think about the day that no one talks about. It will help you to accept your fate and enable you to explore the unexplored! Let's go on this journey together, and let's **Imagine that Today is Your Last Day**

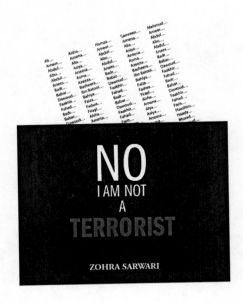

'Terrorism' and 'terrorist' are the latest media buzzwords! However, do you actually know what each of these terms mean? Do you know who a 'terrorist' is? What comes to your mind when you think of a 'terrorist'? Is it a man with a beard, or is it a woman in a veil? Muslims worldwide are being stereotyped and labeled as 'terrorists'. Have you ever stopped and wondered why? Have you ever made the time to discover what lies under the beard and the dress? Have you ever stopped to think what Islam actually has to say about 'terrorism'? Find the answers to all the above questions and more in this book, *'NO! I AM NOT A TERRORIST!'*

Are Muslim Women Oppressed?
Beyond the Veil

Learn about the dignified and well-managed lives of Muslim women and know the reasons why they dress the way they do. *'Are Muslim Women OPPRESSED?'* answers your questions: Why do Muslim women wear those weird clothes? Are they doing it for men? Are they inferior? Do they have no rights? *'Are Muslim Women OPPRESSED?'* will reveal the truth behind the concealed Muslim woman. It is a voyage from behind the veil to the real freedom and will give you an insight about Muslim women like you have never read before. Read and clear the misconceptions; separate the facts from the myths!

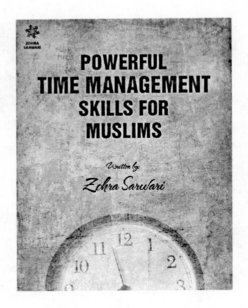

Powerful Time Management Skills For Muslims *will teach you powerful skills which will help you achieve your goals and meet your deadlinesinsha'Allaah. It will guide you from an Islamic perspective, and will teach you how Prophet Muhammad (PBUH) used to spend his time. Each chapter has an activity to follow up on to keep you charged up, which will help you implement what you just read- insha'Allaah.*

This book will help you address your weaknesses step-by-step, and help you convert them into your strengthsinsha'Allaah.

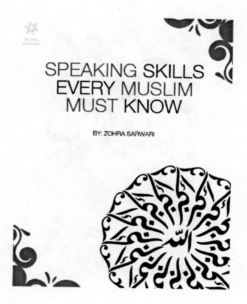

"Speaking Skills Every Muslim Must Know" *is a book which has a collection of tips, tricks, methods and strategies to face the public and deliver your speech in an effective manner. This book is unique as it portrays the Islamic way of becoming a powerful speaker, as Islam was spread through the power of words.*

Who Am I?
Figure Out YOUR Identity

Have you ever wondered who you are? Do you know your strengths and weaknesses? Have you ever wondered who you don't want to be? Have you tried to fit in but couldn't find the right place? **'Who Am I'** is a book that identifies who a Muslim teen is and what characteristics one should possess. It defines who you are and who you want to become. **'Who Am I?'** will take you on a journey that will help you not only discover who you really are, but also strengthen your skills in leadership, time-management and self-esteem insha'Allaah.

The Key Strategies That Can Make Anyone A Successful Leader
Be the Leader Everyone Wants to Follow

The Key Strategies That Can Make Anyone A Successful Leader *is a book for anyone who wants to be an exceptional leader. Oftentimes we wonder if leadership is something inborn or whether it can be acquired through learning. I know that it is something that can be learned. In this book insha'Allaah you will see that leadership can start as early as a child and continue through one's golden years, insha'Allaah. Every person has the urge to lead and has a leader within.*

The Key Strategies That Can Make Anyone A Successful Leader *shares with you some fundamental but crucial strategies which will bring out the leader within you. Learn these key strategies and implement them in your life to become an extraordinary leader, insha'Allaah.*

Special Quantity Discount Offer!

- ► 20-99 books $10.00 per copy
- ► 100-499 books $7.00 each
- ► 500-999 books $5.00 each

Have You Bought The Series, "Things Every Kid Should Know: Smoking, Drugs, Alcohol and Bullying" for Your Kids?

Written By A "9 Year Old" Author
Alya Nuri

www.ThingsEveryKidShouldKnow.com
www.AlyaNuri.com

Things Every Kid Should Know - Drugs!

'Things Every Kid Should Know - Drugs!' *will walk you through what Drugs are; why they are bad for you, and how to avoid picking up this bad habit. There is a story of a young man who goes through his high school doing drugs, and what happens in his life due to making that choice. There are also facts in the story to help understand the issue of Drugs.*

Things Every Kid Should Know - Alcohol!

'Things Every Kid Should Know - Alcohol!' *will walk you through what Alcohol is; why it is bad for you, and how to avoid picking up this bad habit. There is a story of a girl who discovers Alcohol at a friend's house. Her curiosity makes her want to learn more about the topic, but when her friend's dad gets into trouble because of it, she makes a vow. There are also facts in the story to help understand the issues relating to Alcohol.*

Things Every Kid Should Know - Smoking!

'Things Every Kid Should Know - Smoking!' *will walk you through what Smoking is; why it is bad for you, and how to avoid picking up this bad habit. There is a story of two young friends who go through life, and what happens along their lives as they each make different choices. There are also facts in the story to help understand all the issues relating to Smoking.*

Things Every Kid Should Know - Bullying!

'Things Every Kid Should Know - Bullying!' *will walk you through what Bullying is; why it is bad for you, and how to avoid picking up this bad habit. There is a story in this book to help kids learn what Bullying is all about. There are also facts in the story to help understand all the issues relating to Bullying.*

Things Every Kid Should Know - Strangers!

Written By A "6 Year Old" Author
Zafar Nuri

www.ThingsEveryKidShouldKnow.com
www.ZafarNuri.com

'Things Every Kid Should Know - Strangers!' *will walk you through what a Stranger is, why you need to be aware of it, and how to react if you were ever in a situation where you needed help. There is a story of two friends who were about to get kidnapped, but how their actions helped them escape from it! There are also many facts about Strangers to help understand it better.*

CPSIA information can be obtained at www.ICGtesting.com
Printed in the USA
LVOW081319031212

309871LV00001B/33/P